THE ART of WAR

THE ART of WAR

The complete text of Sun Tzu's classic compiled in this special edition with Frederick the Great's *Instructions to His Generals* and Machiavelli's *The Prince*, with an introduction by

GENERAL MARC A. MOORE

SWEET WATER PRESS

The Art of War

Copyright © 2004 Sweetwater Press

Produced by Cliff Road Books

ISBN 1-58173-320-8

Book design by Miles G. Parsons

Printed in the U.S.

Contents

Foreword

Marc Moore, Major General, US Marine Corps, (Ret.)

"The world is a stage on which new actors in new costumes continually perform the same old plays," Jesuit priest Tilman Pesch reflected a half-century ago when writing about individuals and their impact on history. A study of the three men and their thoughts expressed in the following pages validates Father Pesch's musings. The performance of those actors while on stage repeats sound guidance over a 22-century stretch that applies today and tomorrow as well as it did thousands of years ago.

Sun Tzu wrote his treatise *Art of War* in 500 BC and Niccolo Machiavelli wrote *The Prince* in 1513. Frederick the Great wrote *Instructions to His Generals* after extensive campaigning and success in wars from 1740 to 1745. Each writer had a particular writing style that has drawn favorable literary critiques from scholars in subsequent centuries. One Chinese scholar described Sun Tzu as compelling the attention of scholars and literary men. "His essays," this critic wrote, "are terse yet elegant, simple yet profound, perspicuous and eminently practical."

Machiavelli wears the mantle as the founder of political science, although not specifically as a military theorist. His writing style consists of illustrating particular circumstances and doesn't follow any orderly method in expanding his thoughts. He speaks of his belief in the value found in "the knowledge of the actions of great men, acquired by long experience in contemporary affairs, and a continual study of antiquity"—sound advice for any character on the world stage.

Frederick the Great was a closet scholar and philosopher while crown prince. As King of Prussia, and the military genius of his period, his writing style came close to being lyrical poetry at times when he was instructing his generals. When he writes about affording his officers "the most certain opportunity of acquiring glory, rescuing their names from the rust of oblivion," the reader realizes this is no run-of-the-mill king.

The 2,500-year time span covered by these three classics proves significant for two reasons. First, The Art of War also meets criteria as the science of war. In two and a half millennia, the history of warfare has proven a science, since it meets the scientific principles of replication and longitudinal experimentation. A journey through these classics reveals similar replications for waging successful warfare. Additional writings on war published over the centuries reveal the same valid principles. The scientific requirements of replication and successful longitudinal experimentation therefore apply. The second reason focuses on identifying any enterprise as an "art." Such identification comes from subjective conclusions.

Subjectively written, a successful application of the warfare art links the senior military leader in a combat theater to every level of warrior leader down to the lowest ranking leaders in firing holes on the forward edge of the battlefield, or the pilots in cockpits over the battle area. Skillfully applying this coordinated linkage ensures successful warfare outcomes. Based on the experience at each leader's level, the individual's study of the warrior's trade, the feel of the battlefield's pulse, the instinctive capability to draw on the learned combinations and orchestration of combat power—all combine to employ the art of war to ensure success in battle. The professors, theorists, and civilian and military leaders at higher authority levels at detached distances may have extensive knowledge and read extensively about the art of war. The artists of war, however, come from those creating history on the battlefield.

Beyond similar principles and thoughts on warfare, each of the three writers has a singular concept contributing to the art of war. Sun Tzu expressed concern about interference from a ruler who inserts influence and direction upon the military forces. He protests against the ruler's attempts to govern the forces as if they were a civilian organization in the kingdom. Sun Tzu states, "There are commands of the sovereign which must not be obeyed." This statement sounds as though General Douglas MacArthur, long a campaigner and "warlord" in Asia, the Philippines before the Second World War, and Japan after, took Sun Tzu at his word. He found himself sacked by President Truman in 1951, when he tended to ignore the president and Washington military leadership early in the Korean War. But the implication and military tradition that stems from Sun Tzu's statement dictates a different meaning. If the commander cannot in conscience obey the ruler or a superior, the commander must ask for a replacement, resign, or decline to obey and face the consequences.

Machiavelli's particular contribution to the waging of war focuses on his concept of nationalism and a citizen's obligation and dedication to defend the country at all costs. He asserted that a country's armed force should embody a drafted militia—devoted to the state—while serving as a symbol of the nation's capabilities and vitality.

Unfortunately, Machiavelli's efforts over seven years to field a Florentine militia amidst the turmoil of continuous wars on the Italian peninsula met with disaster in 1512, when his newly organized militia army fled in the face of a veteran mercenary army. It was a concept before its time, but he planted the seed for the idea of an integrated Italian nation rather than the geographic maze encompassing many competing principalities and kingdoms.

Prussia's Frederick the Great, although the predominant military artist of his period, spent much of his early princely life secretly collecting a large library and studying music and the classic philosophers while corresponding with the French philosopher, Voltaire. By the time of his coronation, he had evolved into an enlightened monarch with a sense of responsibility for his kingdom and his subjects. Frederick had studied Machiavelli and had written *Antimachiavell*, a rejection of Machiavelli's thoughts on political theory and a discourse on Frederick's ideal of a humanistic ruler. Unlike Machiavelli's extolling of unified nationalism, Frederick never sought to unify German-speaking kingdoms into one nation. Unlike the broad principles proclaimed by Sun Tzu, Frederick elaborates in his Instructions with a military professor's meticulousness about troop formations and dispositions in the minute detail necessary to train leaders for a capable and dominating military force.

Scientific principles, replication, and consensus emerge when reading these three military sages. Certain principles relating to success in war appear consistently in all three men's thoughts and remain the basic cornerstones of winning war in any age.

Additionally, these truisms apply to non-military organizations. For instance, the elements of quality followership—positive attitudes toward assigned tasks and confidence in leadership, the organization, and each other—repeat as key principles for mission success.

All three authors express distrust of hired mercenaries, indicating that serving for money alone dilutes unit cohesion and motivation. Another key principle of all three centers on material resources—the ever-vital "beans, bullets, and bandages"—plus other equipment required to sustain a military campaign. These requirements have obvious application in the successful operation of any organization and husbanding them properly spells success or failure.

Another crucial component involves careful planning and preparing possible alternative courses of action. All planning must include gathering detailed information about the operational environment, such as terrain configurations and trafficability, particularly concerning enemy formations. Modern military intelligence collection enjoys sophisticated technology, but the maxims of these writers still have validity when they address information obtained by agents. Agent reports require confirmation by leaders at all levels who, to succeed, must also conduct their own unit reconnaissance. In the civilian world of today such information planning falls under marketing research. When addressing terrain and competition, this transforms into "location, location, location."

All three writers cite aggressive action as a primary element in operational success. Sun Tzu refers to this characteristic as "combined energy."

Machiavelli emphasized vigorous, forceful action stating, "delay hands the advantage to the opponent." Frederick believed that if a leader has the trust of superiors as a competent commander, he should act forcefully with information concerning the enemy, not waiting for a senior's approval.

All three writers discourage attacks on fortified cities. Each points out the heavy cost in personnel and material resources while slowing the momentum of offensive operations. Each indicates that the destruction of a fortified city doesn't leave a happy surviving populace and requires additional resources to hold and rebuild if so required. A parallel civilian example portrays an organization committing to a complex project, heavy in the expenditure of personnel and material resources, and requiring the splitting off of subordinate organizations to complete the enterprise at the expense of other more advantageous projects. That parallel may seem like a stretch, but many a university MBA case study could apply.

What advantages will come from reading these three classics on the art of warfare? The astute reader will gain timeless insight into proven techniques for honing the development of creative leadership and enlightened followership, enriching capacities in military and civilian organizations for the nation's well-being. For the student of war, business, or any endeavor requiring powerful strategic thinking, the fields cultivated and the soil plowed in these readings will expand both knowledge and application of the art—and the science of—war.

Two old proverbs thrown about in academe a half century ago apply here. "Show me what you read—and I'll show you what you are." And, "You become what you think about." So read on and think about what you are and what character role you want to play, in what costume, on tomorrow's world stage.

Sun Tzu's

Art of War

CHAPTER 1

Laying Plans

Sun Tzu said:

The art of war is of vital importance to the State. It is a matter of life and death, a road either to safety or to ruin. Hence it is a subject of inquiry which can on no account be neglected.

The art of war, then, is governed by five constant factors, to be taken into account in one's deliberations, when seeking to determine the conditions obtaining in the field. These are: The Moral Law; Heaven; Earth; The Commander; Method and Discipline.

The Moral Law causes the people to be in complete accord with their ruler, so that they will follow him regardless of their lives, undismayed by any danger.

Heaven signifies night and day, cold and heat, times and seasons.

Earth comprises distances, great and small; danger and security; open ground and narrow passes; the chances of life and death.

The Commander stands for the virtues of

wisdom, sincerity, benevolence, courage, and strictness.

Method and Discipline are the marshaling of the army in its proper subdivisions, the graduations of rank among the officers, the maintenance of roads by which supplies may reach the army, and the control of military expenditure.

These five heads should be familiar to every general: he who knows them will be victorious; he who knows them not will fail.

Therefore, in your deliberations, when seeking to determine the military conditions, let them be made on the basis of a comparison, in this wise:

Which of the two sovereigns is imbued with the Moral Law?

Which of the two generals has the most ability?

With whom lie the advantages derived from Heaven and Earth?

On which side is discipline most rigorously enforced?

Which army is stronger?

On which side are officers and men more highly trained?

In which army is there the greater constancy both in reward and punishment?

By means of these seven considerations I can

forecast victory or defeat.

The general that hearkens to my counsel and acts upon it, will conquer: let such a one be retained in command! The general that hearkens not to my counsel nor acts upon it, will suffer defeat:—let such a one be dismissed!

While heading the profit of my counsel, avail yourself also of any helpful circumstances over and beyond the ordinary rules.

According as circumstances are favorable, one should modify one's plans.

All warfare is based on deception.

Hence, when able to attack, we must seem unable; when using our forces, we must seem inactive; when we are near, we must make the enemy believe we are far away; when far away, we must make him believe we are near.

Hold out baits to entice the enemy. Feign disorder, and crush him.

If he is secure at all points, be prepared for him. If he is in superior strength, evade him.

If your opponent is of choleric temper, seek to irritate him. Pretend to be weak, that he may grow arrogant.

If he is taking his ease, give him no rest. If his forces are united, separate them.

Attack him where he is unprepared, appear where you are not expected.

These military devices, leading to victory, must not be divulged beforehand.

Now the general who wins a battle makes many calculations in his temple before the battle is fought. The general who loses a battle makes but few calculations beforehand. Thus do many calculations lead to victory, and few calculations to defeat: how much more no calculation at all! It is by attention to this point that I can foresee who is likely to win or lose.

CHAPTER 2

Waging War

SUN TZU SAID:

In the operations of war, where there are in the field a thousand swift chariots, as many heavy chariots, and a hundred thousand mail-clad soldiers, with provisions enough to carry them a thousand li, the expenditure at home and at the front, including entertainment of guests, small items such as glue and paint, and sums spent on chariots and armor, will reach the total of a thousand ounces of silver per day. Such is the cost of raising an army of 100,000 men.

When you engage in actual fighting, if victory is long in coming, then men's weapons will grow dull and their ardor will be damped. If you lay siege to a town, you will exhaust your strength.

Again, if the campaign is protracted, the resources of the State will not be equal to the strain.

Now, when your weapons are dulled, your ardor damped, your strength exhausted and your treasure spent, other chieftains will spring up to take advantage of your extremity. Then no man, however wise, will be able to avert the consequences that must ensue.

Thus, though we have heard of stupid haste in war, cleverness has never been seen associated with long delays.

There is no instance of a country having benefited from prolonged warfare.

It is only one who is thoroughly acquainted with the evils of war that can thoroughly understand the profitable way of carrying it on.

The skillful soldier does not raise a second levy, neither are his supply wagons loaded more than twice.

Bring war material with you from home, but forage on the enemy. Thus the army will have food enough for its needs.

Poverty of the State exchequer causes an army to be maintained by contributions from a distance. Contributing to maintain an army at a distance causes the people to be impoverished.

On the other hand, the proximity of an army causes prices to go up; and high prices cause the people's substance to be drained away.

When their substance is drained away, the peasantry will be afflicted by heavy exactions.

With this loss of substance and exhaustion of strength, the homes of the people will be stripped bare, and three-tenths of their income will be dissipated; while government expenses for broken chariots, worn-out horses, breastplates and helmets, bows and arrows, spears and shields, protective mantles, draught oxen and heavy wagons will amount to four-tenths of its total revenue.

Hence a wise general makes a point of foraging on the enemy. One cartload of the enemy's provisions is equivalent to twenty of one's own, and likewise a single picul of his provender is equivalent to twenty from one's own store.

Now in order to kill the enemy, our men must be roused to anger; that there may be advantage from defeating the enemy, they must have their rewards.

Therefore in chariot fighting, when ten or more chariots have been taken, those should be rewarded who took the first. Our own flags should be substituted for those of the enemy, and the chariots mingled and used in conjunction with ours. The captured soldiers should be kindly treated and kept.

This is called using the conquered foe to augment one's own strength.

In war, then, let your great object be victory, not lengthy campaigns.

Thus it may be known that the leader of
armies is the arbiter of the people's fate, the man
on whom it depends whether the nation shall be
in peace or in peril.

CHAPTER 3

Attack By Stratagem

Sun Tzu said:

In the practical art of war, the best thing of all is to take the enemy's country whole and intact; to shatter and destroy it is not so good. So, too, it is better to recapture an army entire than to destroy it, to capture a regiment, a detachment or a company entire than to destroy them.

Hence to fight and conquer in all your battles is not supreme excellence; supreme excellence consists of breaking the enemy's resistance without fighting.

Thus the highest form of generalship is to balk the enemy's plans; the next best is to prevent the junction of the enemy's forces; the next in order is to attack the enemy's army in the field; and the worst policy of all is to besiege walled cities.

The rule is not to besiege walled cities if it can possibly be avoided. The preparation of mantlets, movable shelters, and various implements of war will take up three whole months; and the piling up of mounds over against the walls will take three months more.

The general, unable to control his irritation, will launch his men to the assault like swarming ants, with the result that one-third of his men are slain, while the town still remains untaken. Such are the disastrous effects of a siege.

Therefore, the skillful leader subdues the enemy's troops without any fighting; he captures their cities without laying siege to them; he overthrows their kingdom without lengthy operations in the field.

With his forces intact he will dispute the mastery of the Empire, and thus, without losing a man, his triumph will be complete. This is the method of attacking by stratagem.

It is the rule in war, if our forces are ten to the enemy's one, to surround him; if five to one, to attack him; if twice as numerous, to divide our army into two.

If equally matched, we can offer battle; if slightly inferior in numbers, we can avoid the enemy; if quite unequal in every way, we can flee from him.

Hence, though an obstinate fight may be made by a small force, in the end it must be captured by the larger force.

Now the general is the bulwark of the State; if

the bulwark is complete at all points, the State will be strong; if the bulwark is defective, the State will be weak.

There are three ways in which a ruler can bring misfortune upon his army:

By commanding the army to advance or to retreat,

being ignorant of the fact that it cannot obey. This is called

hobbling the army.

By attempting to govern an army in the same way as he

administers a kingdom, being ignorant of the conditions

which obtain in an army. This causes restlessness in the

soldier's minds.

By employing the officers of his army without

discrimination, through ignorance of the military

principle of adaptation to circumstances. This shakes the

confidence of the soldiers.

But when the army is restless and distrustful, trouble is sure to come from the other feudal princes. This is simply bringing anarchy into the army, and flinging victory away.

Thus we may know that there are five essentials for victory: He will win who knows when to fight and when not to fight.

He will win who knows how to handle both superior and inferior forces.

He will win whose army is animated by the same spirit throughout all its ranks.

He will win who, prepared himself, waits to take the enemy unprepared.

He will win who has military capacity and is not interfered with by the sovereign.

Hence the saying: If you know the enemy and know yourself, you need not fear the result of a hundred battles. If you know yourself but not the enemy, for every victory gained you will also suffer a defeat. If you know neither the enemy nor yourself, you will succumb in every battle.

CHAPTER 4

Tactical Dispositions

Sun Tzu said:

The good fighters of old first put themselves beyond the possibility of defeat, and then waited for an opportunity of defeating the enemy.

To secure ourselves against defeat lies in our own hands, but the opportunity of defeating the enemy is provided by the enemy himself.

Thus the good fighter is able to secure himself against defeat, but cannot make certain of defeating the enemy.

Hence the saying: One may know how to conquer without being able to do it.

Security against defeat implies defensive tactics; ability to defeat the enemy means taking the offensive.

Standing on the defensive indicates insufficient strength; attacking, a superabundance of strength.

The general who is skilled in defense hides in the most secret recesses of the earth; he who is skilled in attack flashes forth from the topmost heights of heaven. Thus on the one hand, we have the ability to protect ourselves; on the other, a victory that is complete.

To see victory only when it is within the ken of the common herd is not the acme of excellence.

Neither is it the acme of excellence if you fight and conquer and the whole Empire says, "Well done!"

To lift an autumn hare is no sign of great strength; to see the sun and moon is no sign of sharp sight; to hear the noise of thunder is no sign of a quick ear.

What the ancients called a clever fighter is one who not only wins, but excels in winning with ease.

Hence his victories bring him neither reputation for wisdom nor credit for courage.

He wins his battles by making no mistakes. Making no mistakes is what establishes the certainty of victory, for it means conquering an enemy that is already defeated.

Hence the skillful fighter puts himself into a position which makes defeat impossible, and does not miss the moment for defeating the enemy.

Thus it is that in war the victorious strategist only seeks battle after the victory has been won, whereas he who is destined to defeat first fights and afterwards looks for victory.

The consummate leader cultivates the moral law, and strictly adheres to method and discipline; thus it is in his power to control success.

In respect of military method, we have, firstly, Measurement; secondly, Estimation of quantity; thirdly, Calculation; fourthly, Balancing of chances; fifthly, Victory.

Measurement owes its existence to Earth; Estimation of quantity to Measurement; Calculation to Estimation of quantity; Balancing of chances to Calculation; and Victory to Balancing of chances.

A victorious army opposed to a routed one, is as a pound's weight placed in the scale against a single grain.

The onrush of a conquering force is like the bursting of pent-up waters into a chasm a thousand fathoms deep.

CHAPTER 5

Energy

SUN TZU SAID:

The control of a large force is the same principle as the control of a few men: it is merely a question of dividing up their numbers.

Fighting with a large army under your command is nowise different from fighting with a small one: it is merely a question of instituting signs and signals.

To ensure that your whole host may withstand the brunt of the enemy's attack and remain unshaken—this is effected by maneuvers direct and indirect.

That the impact of your army may be like a grindstone dashed against an egg—this is effected by the science of weak points and strong.

In all fighting, the direct method may be used for joining battle, but indirect methods will be needed in order to secure victory.

Indirect tactics, efficiently applied, are as inexhaustible as Heaven and Earth, unending as the flow of rivers and streams; like the sun and moon, they end but to begin anew; like the four seasons, they pass away to return once more.

There are not more than five musical notes, yet the combinations of these five give rise to more melodies than can ever be heard.

There are not more than five primary colors (blue, yellow, red, white, and black), yet in combination they produce more hues than can ever been seen.

There are not more than five cardinal tastes (sour, acrid, salt, sweet, bitter), yet combinations of them yield more flavors than can ever be tasted.

In battle, there are not more than two methods of attack—the direct and the indirect; yet these two in combination give rise to an endless series of maneuvers.

The direct and the indirect lead on to each other in turn. It is like moving in a circle—you never come to an end. Who can exhaust the possibilities of their combination?

The onset of troops is like the rush of a torrent which will even roll stones along in its course.

The quality of decision is like the well-timed swoop of a falcon which enables it to strike and destroy its victim.

Therefore the good fighter will be terrible in his onset, and prompt in his decision.

Energy may be likened to the bending of a

crossbow; decision, to the releasing of a trigger.

Amid the turmoil and tumult of battle, there may be seeming disorder and yet no real disorder at all; amid confusion and chaos, your array may be without head or tail, yet it will be proof against defeat.

Simulated disorder postulates perfect discipline; simulated fear postulates courage; simulated weakness postulates strength.

Hiding order beneath the cloak of disorder is simply a question of subdivision; concealing courage under a show of timidity presupposes a fund of latent energy; masking strength with weakness is to be effected by tactical dispositions.

Thus one who is skillful at keeping the enemy on the move maintains deceitful appearances, according to which the enemy will act. He sacrifices something, that the enemy may snatch at it.

By holding out baits, he keeps him on the march; then with a body of picked men he lies in wait for him.

The clever combatant looks to the effect of combined energy, and does not require too much from individuals. Hence his ability to pick out the right men and utilize combined energy.

When he utilizes combined energy, his fighting men become as it were like unto rolling logs or stones. For it is the nature of a log or stone to remain motionless on level ground, and to move when on a slope; if four-cornered, to come to a standstill, but if round-shaped, to go rolling down.

Thus the energy developed by good fighting men is as the momentum of a round stone rolled down a mountain thousands of feet in height. So much on the subject of energy.

CHAPTER 6

Weak Points and Strong

SUN TZU SAID:

Whoever is first in the field and awaits the coming of the enemy, will be fresh for the fight; whoever is second in the field and has to hasten to battle will arrive exhausted.

Therefore the clever combatant imposes his will on the enemy, but does not allow the enemy's will to be imposed on him.

By holding out advantages to him, he can cause the enemy to approach of his own accord; or, by inflicting damage, he can make it impossible for the enemy to draw near.

If the enemy is taking his ease, he can harass him; if well supplied with food, he can starve him out; if quietly encamped, he can force him to move.

Appear at points which the enemy must hasten to defend; march swiftly to places where you are not expected.

An army may march great distances without distress if it marches through country where the enemy is not.

You can be sure of succeeding in your attacks if you only attack places which are undefended.You can ensure the safety of your defense if you only hold positions that cannot be attacked.

Hence that general is skillful in attack whose opponent does not know what to defend; and he is skillful in defense whose opponent does not know what to attack.

O divine art of subtlety and secrecy! Through you we learn to be invisible, through you inaudible; and hence we can hold the enemy's fate in our hands.

You may advance and be absolutely irresistible, if you make for the enemy's weak points; you may retire and be safe from pursuit if your movements are more rapid than those of the enemy.

If we wish to fight, the enemy can be forced to an engagement even though he be sheltered behind a high rampart and a deep ditch. All we need do is attack some other place that he will be obliged to relieve.

If we do not wish to fight, we can prevent the enemy from engaging us even though the lines of our encampment be merely traced out on the ground. All we need do is to throw something odd and unaccountable in his way.

By discovering the enemy's dispositions and remaining invisible ourselves, we can keep our forces concentrated, while the enemy's must be divided.

We can form a single united body, while the enemy must split up into fractions. Hence there will be a whole pitted against separate parts of a whole, which means that we shall be many to the enemy's few.

And if we are able thus to attack an inferior force with a superior one, our opponents will be in dire straits.

The spot where we intend to fight must not be made known; for then the enemy will have to prepare against a possible attack at several different points; and his forces being thus distributed in many directions, the numbers we shall have to face at any given point will be proportionately few.

For should the enemy strengthen his front, he will weaken his rear; should he strengthen his rear, he will weaken his front; should he strengthen his left, he will weaken his right; should he strengthen his right, he will weaken his left. If he sends reinforcements everywhere, he will everywhere be weak.

Numerical weakness comes from having to

prepare against possible attacks; numerical strength, from compelling our adversary to make these preparations against us.

Knowing the place and the time of the coming battle, we may concentrate from the greatest distances in order to fight.

But if neither time nor place be known, then the left wing will be impotent to succor the right, the right equally impotent to succor the left, the front unable to relieve the rear, or the rear to support the front. How much more so if the furthest portions of the army are anything under a hundred li apart, and even the nearest are separated by several li!

Though according to my estimate the soldiers of Yueh exceed our own in number, that shall advantage them nothing in the matter of victory. I say then that victory can be achieved.

Though the enemy be stronger in numbers, we may prevent him from fighting. Scheme so as to discover his plans and the likelihood of their success.

Rouse him, and learn the principle of his activity or inactivity. Force him to reveal himself, so as to find out his vulnerable spots.

Carefully compare the opposing army with your own, so that you may know where strength is superabundant and where it is deficient.

In making tactical dispositions, the highest pitch you can attain is to conceal them; conceal your dispositions, and you will be safe from the prying of the subtlest spies, from the machinations of the wisest brains.

How victory may be produced for them out of the enemy's own tactics—that is what the multitude cannot comprehend.

All men can see the tactics whereby I conquer, but what none can see is the strategy out of which victory is evolved.

Do not repeat the tactics which have gained you one victory, but let your methods be regulated by the infinite variety of circumstances.

Military tactics are like unto water; for water in its natural course runs away from high places and hastens downward.

So in war, the way is to avoid what is strong and to strike at what is weak.

Water shapes its course according to the nature of the ground over which it flows; the soldier works out his victory in relation to the foe whom he is facing.

Therefore, just as water retains no constant shape, so in warfare there are no constant conditions.

He who can modify his tactics in relation to his opponent and thereby succeed in winning, may be called a heaven-born captain.

The five elements (water, fire, wood, metal, earth) are not always equally predominant; the four seasons make way for each other in turn. There are short days and long; the moon has its periods of waning and waxing.

CHAPTER 7

Maneuvering

Sun Tzu said:

In war, the general receives his commands from the sovereign.

Having collected an army and concentrated his forces, he must blend and harmonize the different elements thereof before pitching his camp.

After that comes tactical maneuvering, than which there is nothing more difficult. The difficulty of tactical maneuvering consists in turning the devious into the direct, and misfortune into gain.

Thus, to take a long and circuitous route, after enticing the enemy out of the way, and though starting after him, to contrive to reach the goal before him, shows knowledge of the artifice of DEVIATION.

Maneuvering with an army is advantageous; with an undisciplined multitude, most dangerous.

If you set a fully equipped army in march in

order to snatch an advantage, the chances are that you will be too late. On the other hand, to detach a flying column for the purpose involves the sacrifice of its baggage and stores.

Thus, if you order your men to roll up their buff-coats, and make forced marches without halting day or night, covering double the usual distance at a stretch, doing a hundred li in order to wrest an advantage, the leaders of all your three divisions will fall into the hands of the enemy.

The stronger men will be in front, the jaded ones will fall behind, and on this plan only one-tenth of your army will reach its destination.

If you march fifty li in order to outmaneuver the enemy, you will lose the leader of your first division, and only half your force will reach the goal.

If you march thirty li with the same object, two-thirds of your army will arrive.

We may take it then that an army without its baggage train is lost; without provisions it is lost; without bases of supply it is lost.

We cannot enter into alliances until we are acquainted with the designs of our neighbors.

We are not fit to lead an army on the march unless we are familiar with the face of the country—its mountains and forests, its pitfalls and precipices, its marshes and swamps.

We shall be unable to turn natural advantage to account unless we make use of local guides.

In war, practice dissimulation, and you will succeed.

Whether to concentrate or to divide your troops, must be decided by circumstances.

Let your rapidity be that of the wind, your compactness that of the forest.

In raiding and plundering be like fire, in immovability, like a mountain.

Let your plans be dark and impenetrable as night, and when you move, fall like a thunderbolt.

When you plunder a countryside, let the spoil be divided amongst your men; when you capture new territory, cut it up into allotments for the benefit of the soldiery.

Ponder and deliberate before you make a move.

He will conquer who has learned the artifice of deviation. Such is the art of maneuvering.

The Book of Army Management says: On the field of battle, the spoken word does not carry far enough: hence the institution of gongs and drums. Nor can ordinary objects be seen clearly enough: hence the institution of banners and flags.

Gongs and drums, banners and flags, are means whereby the ears and eyes of the host may be focused on one particular point.

The host thus forming a single united body, is it impossible either for the brave to advance alone, or for the cowardly to retreat alone. This is the art of handling large masses of men.

In nightfighting, then, make much use of signal fires and drums, and in fighting by day, of flags and banners, as a means of influencing the ears and eyes of your army.

A whole army may be robbed of its spirit; a commander-in-chief may be robbed of his presence of mind.

Now a soldier's spirit is keenest in the morning; by noonday it has begun to flag; and in the evening, his mind is bent only on returning to camp.

A clever general, therefore, avoids an army when its spirit is keen, but attacks it when it is sluggish and inclined to return. This is the art of studying moods.

Disciplined and calm, to await the appearance of disorder and hubbub amongst the enemy— this is the art of retaining self-possession.

To be near the goal while the enemy is still far from it, to wait at ease while the enemy is toiling and struggling, to be well-fed while the enemy is famished—this is the art of husbanding one's strength.

To refrain from intercepting an enemy whose banners are in perfect order, to refrain from attacking an army drawn up in calm and confident array—this is the art of studying circumstances.

It is a military axiom not to advance uphill against the enemy, nor to oppose him when he comes downhill.

Do not pursue an enemy who simulates flight; do not attack soldiers whose temper is keen.

Do not swallow bait offered by the enemy. Do not interfere with an army that is returning home.

When you surround an army, leave an outlet free. Do not press a desperate foe too hard.

Such is the art of warfare.

CHAPTER 8

Variations in Tactics

Sun Tzu said:

In war, the general receives his commands from the sovereign, collects his army, and concentrates his forces.

When in difficult country, do not encamp. In country where high roads intersect, join hands with your allies. Do not linger in dangerously isolated positions. In hemmed-in situations, you must resort to stratagem. In desperate positions, you must fight.

There are roads which must not be followed, armies which must be not attacked, towns which must not be besieged, positions which must not be contested, commands of the sovereign which must not be obeyed.

The general who thoroughly understands the advantages that accompany variation of tactics knows how to handle his troops.

The general who does not understand these may be well acquainted with the configuration of the country, yet he will not be able to turn his knowledge to practical account.

So, the student of war who is unversed in the art of war of varying his plans, even though he be acquainted with the Five Advantages, will fail to make the best use of his men.

Hence, in the wise leader's plans, considerations of advantage and of disadvantage will be blended together.

If our expectation of advantage be tempered in this way, we may succeed in accomplishing the essential part of our schemes.

If, on the other hand, in the midst of difficulties we are always ready to seize an advantage, we may extricate ourselves from misfortune.

Reduce the hostile chiefs by inflicting damage on them; make trouble for them, and keep them constantly engaged; hold out specious allurements and make them rush to any given point.

The art of war teaches us to rely not on the likelihood of the enemy's not coming, but on our own readiness to receive him; not on the chance of his not attacking, but rather on the fact that we have made our position unassailable.

There are five dangerous faults which may affect a general:

Recklessness, which leads to destruction;

cowardice, which leads to capture;

a hasty temper, which can be provoked by insults;

a delicacy of honor which is sensitive to shame;

oversolicitude for his men, which exposes him to worry and trouble.

These are the five besetting sins of a general, ruinous to the conduct of war.

When an army is overthrown and its leader slain, the cause will surely be found among these five dangerous faults. Let them be a subject of meditation.

CHAPTER 9

The Army on the March

SUN TZU SAID:

We come now to the question of encamping the army, and observing signs of the enemy. Pass quickly over mountains, and keep in the neighborhood of valleys.

Camp in high places, facing the sun. Do not climb heights in order to fight. So much for mountain warfare.

After crossing a river, you should get far away from it.

When an invading force crosses a river in its onward march, do not advance to meet it in midstream. It will be best to let half the army get across, and then deliver your attack.

If you are anxious to fight, you should not go to meet the invader near a river which he has to cross.

Moor your craft higher up than the enemy, and facing the sun. Do not move upstream to meet the enemy. So much for river warfare.

In crossing salt-marshes, your sole concern

should be to get over them quickly, without any delay.

If forced to fight in a salt marsh, you should have water and grass near you, and get your back to a clump of trees. So much for operations in salt marshes.

In dry, level country, take up an easily accessible position with rising ground to your right and at your rear, so that the danger may be in front, and safety lie behind. So much for campaigning in flat country.

These are the four useful branches of military knowledge which enabled the Yellow Emperor to vanquish four sovereigns.

All armies prefer high ground to low and sunny places to dark.

If you are careful of your men, and camp on hard ground, the army will be free from disease of every kind, and this will spell victory.

When you come to a hill or a bank, occupy the sunny side, with the slope on your right rear. Thus you will at once act for the benefit of your soldiers and utilize the natural advantages of the ground.

When, in consequence of heavy rains up-country, a river which you wish to ford is swollen and flecked with foam, you must wait until it subsides.

Country in which there are precipitous cliffs with torrents running between, deep natural hollows, confined places, tangled thickets, quagmires, and crevasses, should be left with all possible speed and not approached.

While we keep away from such places, we should get the enemy to approach them; while we face them, we should let the enemy have them on his rear.

If in the neighborhood of your camp there should be any hilly country, ponds surrounded by aquatic grass, hollow basins filled with reeds, or woods with thick undergrowth, they must be carefully routed out and searched; for these are places where men in ambush or insidious spies are likely to be lurking.

When the enemy is close at hand and remains quiet, he is relying on the natural strength of his position.

When he keeps aloof and tries to provoke a battle, he is anxious for the other side to advance.

If his place of encampment is easy of access, he is tendering a bait.

Movement amongst the trees of a forest shows that the enemy is advancing. The appearance of a number of screens in the midst of thick grass means that the enemy wants to make us suspicious.

The rising of birds in their flight is the sign of an ambush. Startled beasts indicate that a sudden attack is coming.

When there is dust rising in a high column, it is the sign of chariots advancing; when the dust is low, but spread over a wide area, it betokens the approach of infantry. When it branches out in different directions, it shows that parties have been sent to collect firewood. A few clouds of dust moving to and fro signify that the army is encamping.

Humble words and increased preparations are signs that the enemy is about to advance. Violent language and driving forward as if to the attack are signs that he will retreat.

When the light chariots come out first and take up a position on the wings, it is a sign that the enemy is forming for battle.

Peace proposals unaccompanied by a sworn covenant indicate a plot.

When there is much running about and the soldiers fall into rank, it means that the critical moment has come.

When some are seen advancing and some retreating, it is a lure.

When the soldiers stand leaning on their spears, they are faint from want of food.

If those who are sent to draw water begin by

drinking themselves, the army is suffering from thirst.

If the enemy sees an advantage to be gained and makes no effort to secure it, the soldiers are exhausted.

If birds gather on any spot, it is unoccupied. Clamor by night betokens nervousness.

If there is disturbance in the camp, the general's authority is weak. If the banners and flags are shifted about, sedition is afoot. If the officers are angry, it means that the men are weary.

When an army feeds its horses with grain and kills its cattle for food, and when the men do not hang their cooking pots over the campfires, showing that they will not return to their tents, you may know that they are determined to fight to the death.

The sight of men whispering together in small knots or speaking in subdued tones points to disaffection amongst the rank and file.

Too frequent rewards signify that the enemy is at the end of his resources; too many punishments betray a condition of dire distress.

To begin by bluster, but afterwards to take fright at the enemy's numbers, shows a supreme lack of intelligence.

When envoys are sent with compliments in

their mouths, it is a sign that the enemy wishes for a truce.

If the enemy's troops march up angrily and remain facing ours for a long time without either joining battle or taking themselves off again, the situation is one that demands great vigilance and circumspection.

If our troops are no more in number than the enemy, that is amply sufficient; it only means that no direct attack can be made. What we can do is simply to concentrate all our available strength, keep a close watch on the enemy, and obtain reinforcements.

He who exercises no forethought but makes light of his opponents is sure to be captured by them.

If soldiers are punished before they have grown attached to you, they will not prove submissive; and, unless submissive, they will be practically useless. If, when the soldiers have become attached to you, punishments are not enforced, they will still be useless.

Therefore soldiers must be treated in the first instance with humanity, but kept under control by means of iron discipline. This is a certain road to victory.

If in training soldiers' commands are habitually enforced, the army will be well-disciplined; if not, its discipline will be bad.

If a general shows confidence in his men but always insists on his orders being obeyed, the gain will be mutual.

CHAPTER 10

Terrain

Sun Tzu said:

We may distinguish six kinds of terrain, to wit:
Accessible ground;
entangling ground;
temporizing ground;
narrow passes;
precipitous heights;
positions at a great distance from the enemy.

Ground which can be freely traversed by both sides is called accessible.

With regard to ground of this nature, be before the enemy in occupying the raised and sunny spots, and carefully guard your line of supplies. Then you will be able to fight with advantage.

Ground which can be abandoned but is hard to reoccupy is called entangling.

From a position of this sort, if the enemy is unprepared, you may sally forth and defeat him. But if the enemy is prepared for your coming, and you fail to defeat him, then, return being impossible, disaster will ensue.

When the position is such that neither side will gain by making the first move, it is called temporizing ground.

In a position of this sort, even though the enemy should offer us an attractive bait, it will be advisable not to stir forth, but rather to retreat, thus enticing the enemy in his turn; then, when part of his army has come out, we may deliver our attack with advantage.

With regard to narrow passes, if you can occupy them first, let them be strongly garrisoned and await the advent of the enemy.

Should the army forestall you in occupying a pass, do not go after him if the pass is fully garrisoned, but only if it is weakly garrisoned.

With regard to precipitous heights, if you are beforehand with your adversary, you should occupy the raised and sunny spots, and there wait for him to come up.

If the enemy has occupied them before you, do not follow him, but retreat and try to entice him away.

If you are situated at a great distance from the enemy, and the strength of the two armies is equal, it is not easy to provoke a battle, and fighting will be to your disadvantage.

These six are the principles connected with

Earth. The general who has attained a responsible post must be careful to study them.

Now an army is exposed to six several calamities, not arising from natural causes, but from faults for which the general is responsible. These are: Flight; insubordination; collapse; ruin; disorganization; rout.

Other conditions being equal, if one force is hurled against another ten times its size, the result will be the flight of the former.

When the common soldiers are too strong and their officers too weak, the result is insubordination. When the officers are too strong and the common soldiers too weak, the result is collapse.

When the higher officers are angry and insubordinate, and on meeting the enemy give battle on their own account from a feeling of resentment, before the commander-in-chief can tell whether or not he is in a position to fight, the result is ruin.

When the general is weak and without authority; when his orders are not clear and distinct; when there are no fixed duties assigned to officers and men, and the ranks are formed in a slovenly haphazard manner, the result is utter disorganization.

When a general, unable to estimate the

enemy's strength, allows an inferior force to engage a larger one, or hurls a weak detachment against a powerful one, and neglects to place picked soldiers in the front rank, the result must be rout.

These are six ways of courting defeat, which must be carefully noted by the general who has attained a responsible post.

The natural formation of the country is the soldier's best ally; but a power of estimating the adversary, of controlling the forces of victory, and of shrewdly calculating difficulties, dangers and distances, constitutes the test of a great general.

He who knows these things, and in fighting puts his knowledge into practice, will win his battles. He who knows them not, nor practices them, will surely be defeated.

If fighting is sure to result in victory, then you must fight, even though the ruler forbid it; if fighting will not result in victory, then you must not fight even at the ruler's bidding.

The general who advances without coveting fame and retreats without fearing disgrace, whose only thought is to protect his country and do good service for his sovereign, is the jewel of the kingdom.

Regard your soldiers as your children, and they will follow you into the deepest valleys;

look upon them as your own beloved sons, and they will stand by you even unto death.

If, however, you are indulgent, but unable to make your authority felt; kind-hearted, but unable to enforce your commands; and incapable, moreover, of quelling disorder, then your soldiers must be likened to spoilt children; they are useless for any practical purpose.

If we know that our own men are in a condition to attack, but are unaware that the enemy is not open to attack, we have gone only halfway towards victory.

If we know that the enemy is open to attack, but are unaware that our own men are not in a condition to attack, we have gone only halfway towards victory.

If we know that the enemy is open to attack, and also know that our men are in a condition to attack, but are unaware that the nature of the ground makes fighting impracticable, we have still gone only halfway towards victory.

Hence the experienced soldier, once in motion, is never bewildered; once he has broken camp, he is never at a loss.

Hence the saying: If you know the enemy and know yourself, your victory will not stand in doubt; if you know Heaven and know Earth, you may make your victory complete.

CHAPTER 11

The Nine Situations

SUN TZU SAID:

The art of war recognizes nine varieties of ground:
Dispersive ground
Facile ground
Contentious ground
Open ground
Ground of intersecting highways
Serious ground
Difficult ground
Hemmed-in ground
Desperate ground.

When a chieftain is fighting in his own territory, it is dispersive ground.

When he has penetrated into hostile territory, but to no great distance, it is facile ground.

Ground the possession of which imports great advantage to either side, is contentious ground.

Ground on which each side has liberty of movement is open ground.

Ground which forms the key to three contiguous states, so that he who occupies it first has most of the Empire at his command, is a ground of intersecting highways.

When an army has penetrated into the heart of a hostile country, leaving a number of fortified cities in its rear, it is serious ground.

Mountain forests, rugged steeps, marshes and wetlands—all country that is hard to traverse: this is difficult ground.

Ground which is reached through narrow gorges, and from which we can only retire by tortuous paths, so that a small number of the enemy would suffice to crush a large body of our men: this is hemmed-in ground.

Ground on which we can only be saved from destruction by fighting without delay is desperate ground.

On dispersive ground, therefore, fight not. On facile ground, halt not. On contentious ground, attack not.

On open ground, do not try to block the enemy's way. On the ground of intersecting highways, join hands with your allies.

On serious ground, gather in plunder. In difficult ground, keep steadily on the march.

On hemmed-in ground, resort to stratagem. On desperate ground, fight.

Those who were called skillful leaders of old knew how to drive a wedge between the enemy's front and rear; to prevent cooperation between his large and small divisions; to hinder the good troops from rescuing the bad, the officers from rallying their men.

When the enemy's men were united, they managed to keep them in disorder.

When it was to their advantage, they made a forward move; when otherwise, they stopped still.

Regarding how to cope with a great host of the enemy in orderly array and on the point of marching to the attack, begin by seizing something which your opponent holds dear; then he will be amenable to your will.

Rapidity is the essence of war: take advantage of the enemy's unreadiness, make your way by unexpected routes, and attack unguarded spots.

The following are the principles to be observed by an invading force: The farther you penetrate into a country, the greater will be the solidarity of your troops, and thus the defenders will not prevail against you.

Make forays in fertile country in order to supply your army with food.

Carefully study the well-being of your men, and do not overtax them. Concentrate your energy and hoard your strength. Keep your army continually on the move, and devise unfathomable plans.

Throw your soldiers into positions whence there is no escape, and they will prefer death to flight. If they will face death, there is nothing they may not achieve. Officers and men alike will put forth their uttermost strength.

Soldiers when in desperate straits lose the sense of fear. If there is no place of refuge, they will stand firm. If they are in hostile country, they will show a stubborn front. If there is no help for it, they will fight hard.

Thus, without waiting to be marshaled, the soldiers will be constantly on the ready; without waiting to be asked, they will do your will; without restrictions, they will be faithful; without giving orders, they can be trusted.

Prohibit the taking of omens, and do away with superstitious doubts. Then, until death itself comes, no calamity need be feared.

If our soldiers are not overburdened with money, it is not because they have a distaste for riches; if their lives are not unduly long, it is not because they are disinclined to longevity.

On the day they are ordered out to battle, your soldiers may weep, those sitting up bedewing their garments, and those lying down letting the tears run down their cheeks. But let them once be brought to bay, and they will display the courage of a Chu or a Kuei.

The skillful tactician may be likened to the shuai-jan. Now the shuai-jan is a snake that is found in the Chung mountains. Strike at its head, and you will be attacked by its tail; strike at its tail, and you will be attacked by its head; strike at its middle, and you will be attacked by head and tail both.

Asked if an army can be made to imitate the shuai-jan, I should answer yes. For the men of Wu and the men of Yueh are enemies; yet if they are crossing a river in the same boat and are caught by a storm, they will come to each other's assistance just as the left hand helps the right.

Hence it is not enough to put one's trust in the tethering of horses, and the burying of chariot wheels in the ground

The principle on which to manage an army is to set up one standard of courage which all must reach.

How to make the best of both strong and weak—that is a question involving the proper use of ground.

Thus the skillful general conducts his army just as though he were leading a single man, willy-nilly, by the hand.

It is the business of a general to be quiet and

thus ensure secrecy; upright and just, and thus maintain order.

He must be able to mystify his officers and men by false reports and appearances, and thus keep them in total ignorance.

By altering his arrangements and changing his plans, he keeps the enemy without definite knowledge. By shifting his camp and taking circuitous routes, he prevents the enemy from anticipating his purpose.

At the critical moment, the leader of an army acts like one who has climbed up a height and then kicks away the ladder behind him. He carries his men deep into hostile territory before he shows his hand.

He burns his boats and breaks his cooking pots; like a shepherd driving a flock of sheep, he drives his men this way and that, and no one knows whither he is going.

To muster his host and bring it into danger— this may be termed the business of the general.

The different measures suited to the nine varieties of ground; the expediency of aggressive or defensive tactics; and the fundamental laws of human nature: these are things that must most certainly be studied.

When invading hostile territory, the general principle is that penetrating deeply brings cohesion; penetrating but a short way means dispersion.

When you leave your own country behind, and take your army across neighboring territory, you find yourself on critical ground. When there are means of communication on all four sides, the ground is one of intersecting highways.

When you penetrate deeply into a country, it is serious ground. When you penetrate but a little way, it is facile ground.

When you have the enemy's strongholds on your rear, and narrow passes in front, it is hemmed-in ground. When there is no place of refuge at all, it is desperate ground.

Therefore, on dispersive ground, I would inspire my men with unity of purpose. On facile ground, I would see that there is close connection between all parts of my army.

On contentious ground, I would hurry up my rear.

On open ground, I would keep a vigilant eye on my defenses. On ground of intersecting highways, I would consolidate my alliances.

On serious ground, I would try to ensure a continuous stream of supplies. On difficult ground, I would keep pushing on along the road.

On hemmed-in ground, I would block any way of retreat. On desperate ground, I would proclaim to my soldiers the hopelessness of saving their lives.

For it is the soldier's disposition to offer an obstinate resistance when surrounded, to fight hard when he cannot help himself, and to obey promptly when he has fallen into danger.

We cannot enter into alliance with neighboring princes until we are acquainted with their designs. We are not fit to lead an army on the march unless we are familiar with the face of the country—its mountains and forests, its pitfalls and precipices, its marshes and swamps. We shall be unable to turn natural advantages to account unless we make use of local guides.

To be ignorant of any one of the following four or five principles does not befit a warlike prince.

When a warlike prince attacks a powerful state, his generalship shows itself in preventing the concentration of the enemy's forces. He overawes his opponents, and their allies are prevented from joining against him.

Hence he does not strive to ally himself with all and sundry, nor does he foster the power of other states. He carries out his own secret designs, keeping his antagonists in awe. Thus he is able to capture their cities and overthrow their kingdoms.

Bestow rewards without regard to rule, issue orders without regard to previous arrangements, and you will be able to handle a whole army as though you had to do with but a single man.

Confront your soldiers with the deed itself; never let them know your design. When the outlook is bright, bring it before their eyes; but tell them nothing when the situation is gloomy.

Place your army in deadly peril, and it will survive; plunge it into desperate straits, and it will come off in safety.

For it is precisely when a force has fallen into harm's way that it is capable of striking a blow for victory.

Success in warfare is gained by carefully accommodating ourselves to the enemy's purpose.

By persistently hanging on the enemy's flank, we shall succeed in the long run in killing the commander-in-chief.

This is called ability to accomplish a thing by sheer cunning.

On the day that you take up your command, block the frontier passes, destroy the official tallies, and stop the passage of all emissaries.

Be stern in the council chamber, so that you may control the situation.

If the enemy leaves a door open, you must rush in.

Forestall your opponent by seizing what he holds dear, and subtly contrive to time his arrival on the ground.

Walk in the path defined by rule, and accommodate yourself to the enemy until you can fight a decisive battle.

At first, then, exhibit the coyness of a maiden, until the enemy gives you an opening; afterwards emulate the rapidity of a running hare, and it will be too late for the enemy to oppose you.

CHAPTER 12

The Attack by Fire

Sun Tzu said:

There are five ways of attacking with fire. The first is to burn soldiers in their camp; the second is to burn stores; the third is to burn baggage trains; the fourth is to burn arsenals and magazines; the fifth is to hurl dropping fire amongst the enemy.

In order to carry out an attack, we must have means available. The material for raising fire should always be kept in readiness.

There is a proper season for making attacks with fire, and special days for starting a conflagration.

The proper season is when the weather is very dry; the special days are those when the moon is in the constellations of the Sieve, the Wall, the Wing or the Cross-bar; for these four are all days of rising wind.

In attacking with fire, one should be prepared to meet five possible developments:

When fire breaks out inside the enemy's

camp, respond at once with an attack from without.

If there is an outbreak of fire, but the enemy's soldiers remain quiet, bide your time and do not attack.

When the force of the flames has reached its height, follow it up with an attack, if that is practicable; if not, stay where you are.

If it is possible to make an assault with fire from without, do not wait for it to break out within, but deliver your attack at a favorable moment.

When you start a fire, be windward of it. Do not attack from the leeward.

A wind that rises in the daytime lasts long, but a night breeze soon falls.

In every army, the five developments connected with fire must be known, the movements of the stars calculated, and a watch kept for the proper days.

Hence those who use fire as an aid to the attack show intelligence; those who use water as an aid to the attack gain an accession of strength.

By means of water, an enemy may be intercepted, but not robbed of all his belongings.

Unhappy is the fate of one who tries to win his battles and succeed in his attacks without cultivating the spirit of enterprise; for the result is waste of time and general stagnation.

Hence the saying: The enlightened ruler lays his plans well ahead; the good general cultivates his resources.

Move not unless you see an advantage; use not your troops unless there is something to be gained; fight not unless the position is critical.

No ruler should put troops into the field merely to gratify his own spleen; no general should fight a battle simply out of pique.

If it is to your advantage, make a forward move; if not, stay where you are.

Anger may in time change to gladness; vexation may be succeeded by content.

But a kingdom that has once been destroyed can never come again into being; nor can the dead ever be brought back to life.

Hence the enlightened ruler is heedful, and the good general full of caution. This is the way to keep a country at peace and an army intact.

CHAPTER 13

The Use of Spies

SUN TZU SAID:

Raising a host of a hundred thousand men and marching them great distances entails heavy loss on the people and a drain on the resources of the State. The daily expenditure will amount to a thousand ounces of silver. There will be commotion at home and abroad, and men will drop down exhausted on the highways. As many as seven hundred thousand families will be impeded in their labor.

Hostile armies may face each other for years, striving for the victory which is decided in a single day. This being so, to remain in ignorance of the enemy's condition simply because one grudges the outlay of a hundred ounces of silver in honors and emoluments, is the height of inhumanity.

One who acts thus is no leader of men, no present help to his sovereign, no master of victory.

Thus, what enables the wise sovereign and

the good general to strike and conquer, and achieve things beyond the reach of ordinary men, is foreknowledge.

Now this foreknowledge cannot be elicited from spirits; it cannot be obtained inductively from experience, nor by any deductive calculation.

Knowledge of the enemy's dispositions can only be obtained from other men.

Hence the use of spies, of whom there are five classes: (1) Local spies; (2) inward spies; (3) converted spies; (4) doomed spies; (5) surviving spies.

When these five kinds of spy are all at work, none can discover the secret system. This is called "divine manipulation of the threads." It is the sovereign's most precious faculty.

Having local spies means employing the services of the inhabitants of a district.

Having inward spies means making use of officials of the enemy.

Having converted spies means getting hold of the enemy's spies and using them for our own purposes.

Having doomed spies means doing certain things openly for purposes of deception, and allowing our spies to know of them and report them to the enemy.

Surviving spies, finally, are those who bring back news from the enemy's camp.

Hence it is that which none in the whole army are more intimate relations to be maintained than with spies. None should be more liberally rewarded. In no other business should greater secrecy be preserved.

Spies cannot be usefully employed without a certain intuitive sagacity.

They cannot be properly managed without benevolence and straightforwardness.

Without subtle ingenuity of mind, one cannot make certain of the truth of their reports.

Be subtle! be subtle! and use your spies for every kind of business.

If a secret piece of news is divulged by a spy before the time is ripe, he must be put to death together with the man to whom the secret was told.

Whether the object be to crush an army, to storm a city, or to assassinate an individual, it is always necessary to begin by finding out the names of the attendants, the aides-de-camp, and doorkeepers and sentries of the general in command. Our spies must be commissioned to ascertain these.

The enemy's spies who have come to spy on us must be sought out, tempted with bribes, led away, and comfortably housed. Thus they will become converted spies and available for our service.

It is through the information brought by the converted spy that we are able to acquire and employ local and inward spies.

It is owing to his information, again, that we can cause the doomed spy to carry false tidings to the enemy.

Lastly, it is by his information that the surviving spy can be used on appointed occasions.

The end and aim of spying in all its five varieties is knowledge of the enemy; and this knowledge can only be derived, in the first instance, from the converted spy. Hence it is essential that the converted spy be treated with the utmost liberality.

Of old, the rise of the Yin dynasty was due to I Chih who had served under the Hsia. Likewise, the rise of the Chou dynasty was due to Lu Ya who had served under the Yin.

Hence, it is only the enlightened ruler and the wise general who will use the highest intelligence of the army for purposes of spying and thereby achieve great results. Spies are a most important element in water, because on them depends an army's ability to move.

Tu Mu closes with a note of warning: "Just as water, which carries a boat from bank to bank, may also be the means of sinking it, so reliance on spies, while production of great results, is oft-times the cause of utter destruction."

Spies are a most important element in water, because on them depends an army's ability to move. Chia Lin says that an army without spies is like a man without ears or eyes.

The Prince

Niccolo Machiavelli

To the Magnificent Lorenzo di Piero De' Medici: Those who strive to obtain the good graces of a prince are accustomed to come before him with such things as they hold most precious, or in which they see him take most delight; whence one often sees horses, arms, cloth of gold, precious stones, and similar ornaments presented to princes, worthy of their greatness. Desiring therefore to present myself to your Magnificence with some testimony of my devotion towards you, I have not found among my possessions anything which I hold more dear than, or value so much as, the knowledge of the actions of great men, acquired by long experience in contemporary affairs, and a continual study of antiquity; which, having reflected upon it with great and prolonged diligence, I now send, digested into a little volume, to your Magnificence.

And although I may consider this work unworthy of your countenance, nevertheless I trust much to your benignity that it may be acceptable, seeing that it is not possible for me to make a better gift than to offer you the opportunity of understanding in the shortest time all that I have learned in so many years, and with so many troubles and dangers; which work I have not embellished with swelling or magnificent words, nor stuffed with rounded periods, nor with any extrinsic allurements or adornments whatever, with which so many are accustomed to embellish their works; for I have wished either that no honor should be given it, or else that the truth of the matter and the weightiness of the theme shall make it acceptable.

Nor do I hold with those who regard it as a presumption if a man of low and humble condition dare to discuss and settle the concerns of princes; because, just as those who draw landscapes place themselves below in the plain to contemplate the nature of the mountains and of lofty places, and in order to contemplate the plains place themselves upon high mountains, even so to understand the nature of the people it needs to be a prince, and to understand that if princes it needs to be of the people.

Take then, your Magnificence, this little gift in the spirit in which I send it; wherein, if it be diligently read and considered by you, you will learn my extreme desire that you should attain that greatness which fortune and your other attributes promise. And if your Magnificence from the summit of your greatness will sometimes turn your eyes to these lower regions, you will see how unmeritedly I suffer a great and continued malignity of fortune.

CHAPTER 1

How Many Kinds of Principalities There Are, and by What Means They Are Acquired

All states, all powers, that have held and hold rule over men have been and are either republics or principalities.

Principalities are either hereditary, in which the family has been long established; or they are new.

The new are either entirely new, as was Milan to Francesco Sforza, or they are, as it were, members annexed to the hereditary state of the prince who has acquired them, as was the kingdom of Naples to that of the King of Spain.

Such dominions thus acquired are either accustomed to live under a prince, or to live in freedom; and are acquired either by the arms of the prince himself, or of others, or else by fortune or by ability.

CHAPTER 2

Concerning Hereditary Principalities

I will leave out all discussion on republics, inasmuch as in another place I have written of them at length, and will address myself only to principalities. In doing so I will keep to the order indicated above, and discuss how such principalities are to be ruled and preserved.

I say at once there are fewer difficulties in holding hereditary states, and those long accustomed to the family of their prince, than new ones; for it is sufficient only not to transgress the customs of his ancestors, and to deal prudently with circumstances as they arise, for a prince of average powers to maintain himself in his state, unless he be deprived of it by some extraordinary and excessive force; and if he should be so deprived of it, whenever anything sinister happens to the usurper, he will regain it.

We have in Italy, for example, the Duke of Ferrara, who could not have withstood the attacks of the Venetians in '84, nor those of Pope

Julius in '10, unless he had been long established in his dominions. For the hereditary prince has less cause and less necessity to offend; hence it happens that he will be more loved; and unless extraordinary vices cause him to be hated, it is reasonable to expect that his subjects will be naturally well disposed towards him; and in the antiquity and duration of his rule the memories and motives that make for change are lost, for one change always leaves the toothing for another.

CHAPTER 3

Concerning Mixed Principalities

But the difficulties occur in a new principality. And firstly, if it be not entirely new, but is, as it were, a member of a state which, taken collectively, may be called composite, the changes arise chiefly from an inherent difficulty which there is in all new principalities; for men change their rulers willingly, hoping to better themselves, and this hope induces them to take up arms against him who rules: wherein they are deceived, because they afterwards find by experience they have gone from bad to worse. This follows also on another natural and common necessity, which always causes a new prince to burden those who have submitted to him with his soldiery and with infinite other hardships which he must put upon his new acquisition. In this way you have enemies in all those whom you have injured in seizing that principality, and you are not able to keep those friends who put you there because of your not being able to satisfy them in the way they expected, and you cannot take strong measures against them, feeling bound to them. For, although one may be very strong in armed forces, yet in entering a province one has always need of the goodwill of the natives.

For these reasons Louis the Twelfth, King of France, quickly occupied Milan, and as quickly lost it; and to turn him out the first time it only needed Lodovico's own forces; because those who had opened the gates to him, finding themselves deceived in their hopes of future benefit, would not endure the ill-treatment of the new prince. It is very true that, after acquiring rebellious provinces a second time, they are not so lightly lost afterwards, because the prince, with little reluctance, takes the opportunity of the rebellion to punish the delinquents, to clear out the suspects, and to strengthen himself in the weakest places. Thus to cause France to lose Milan the first time it was enough for the Duke Lodovico to raise insurrections on the borders; but to cause him to lose it a second time it was necessary to bring the whole world against him, and that his armies should be defeated and driven out of Italy; which followed from the causes above mentioned.

Nevertheless Milan was taken from France

both the first and the second time. The general
reasons for the first have been discussed; it
remains to name those for the second, and to see
what resources he had, and what any one in his
situation would have had for maintaining
himself more securely in his acquisition than did
the King of France. Now I say that those
dominions which, when acquired, are added to
an ancient state by him who acquires them, are
either of the same country and language, or they
are not. When they are, it is easier to hold them,
especially when they have not been accustomed
to self-government; and to hold them securely it
is enough to have destroyed the family of the
prince who was ruling them; because the two
peoples, preserving in other things the old
conditions, and not being unlike in customs, will
live quietly together, as one has seen in Brittany,
Burgundy, Gascony, and Normandy, which have
been bound to France for so long a time: and,
although there may be some difference in
language, nevertheless the customs are alike, and
the people will easily be able to get on amongst
themselves. He who has annexed them, if he
wishes to hold them, has only to bear in mind
two considerations: the one, that the family of
their former lord is extinguished; the other, that
neither their laws nor their taxes are altered, so

that in a very short time they will become entirely one body with the old principality.

But when states are acquired in a country differing in language, customs, or laws, there are difficulties, and good fortune and great energy are needed to hold them, and one of the greatest and most real helps would be that he who has acquired them should go and reside there. This would make his position more secure and durable, as it has made that of the Turk in Greece, who, notwithstanding all the other measures taken by him for holding that state, if he had not settled there, would not have been able to keep it. Because, if one is on the spot, disorders are seen as they spring up, and one can quickly remedy them; but if one is not at hand, they are heard of only when they are great, and then one can no longer remedy them. Besides this, the country is not pillaged by your officials; the subjects are satisfied by prompt recourse to the prince; thus, wishing to be good, they have more cause to love him, and wishing to be otherwise, to fear him. He who would attack that state from the outside must have the utmost caution; as long as the prince resides there it can only be wrested from him with the greatest difficulty.

The other and better course is to send colonies

to one or two places, which may be as keys to that state, for it is necessary either to do this or else to keep there a great number of cavalry and infantry. A prince does not spend much on colonies, for with little or no expense he can send them out and keep them there, and he offends a minority only of the citizens from whom he takes lands and houses to give them to the new inhabitants; and those whom he offends, remaining poor and scattered, are never able to injure him; whilst the rest being uninjured are easily kept quiet, and at the same time are anxious not to err for fear it should happen to them as it has to those who have been despoiled. In conclusion, I say that these colonies are not costly, they are more faithful, they injure less, and the injured, as has been said, being poor and scattered, cannot hurt. Upon this, one has to remark that men ought either to be well treated or crushed, because they can avenge themselves of lighter injuries, of more serious ones they cannot; therefore the injury that is to be done to a man ought to be of such a kind that one does not stand in fear of revenge.

But in maintaining armed men there in place of colonies one spends much more, having to consume on the garrison all the income from the state, so that the acquisition turns into a loss, and

many more are exasperated, because the whole
state is injured; through the shifting of the
garrison up and down all become acquainted with
hardship, and all become hostile, and they are
enemies who, whilst beaten on their own ground,
are yet able to do hurt. For every reason, therefore,
such guards are as useless as a colony is useful.

Again, the prince who holds a country
differing in the above respects ought to make
himself the head and defender of his less
powerful neighbors, and to weaken the more
powerful amongst them, taking care that no
foreigner as powerful as himself shall, by any
accident, get a footing there; for it will always
happen that such a one will be introduced by
those who are discontented, either through excess
of ambition or through fear, as one has seen
already. The Romans were brought into Greece
by the Aetolians; and in every other country
where they obtained a footing they were brought
in by the inhabitants. And the usual course of
affairs is that, as soon as a powerful foreigner
enters a country, all the subject states are drawn
to him, moved by the hatred which they feel
against the ruling power. So that in respect to
those subject states he has not to take any trouble
to gain them over to himself, for the whole of
them quickly rally to the state which he has

acquired there. He has only to take care that they do not get hold of too much power and too much authority, and then with his own forces, and with their goodwill, he can easily keep down the more powerful of them, so as to remain entirely master in the country. And he who does not properly manage this business will soon lose what he has acquired, and whilst he does hold it he will have endless difficulties and troubles.

The Romans, in the countries which they annexed, observed closely these measures; they sent colonies and maintained friendly relations with the minor powers, without increasing their strength; they kept down the greater, and did not allow any strong foreign powers to gain authority. Greece appears to me sufficient for an example. The Achaeans and Aetolians were kept friendly by them, the kingdom of Macedonia was humbled, Antiochus was driven out; yet the merits of the Achaeans and Aetolians never secured for them permission to increase their power, nor did the persuasions of Philip ever induce the Romans to be his friends without first humbling him, nor did the influence of Antiochus make them agree that he should retain any lordship over the country. Because the Romans did in these instances what all prudent princes ought to do, who have to regard not only present troubles, but also future ones, for which they must prepare with every energy, because, when foreseen, it is easy to remedy them; but if you wait until they approach, the medicine is no longer in time because the malady has become incurable; for it happens in this, as the physicians say it happens in hectic fever, that in the beginning of the malady it is easy to cure but difficult to detect, but in the course of time, not having been either detected or treated in the beginning, it becomes easy to detect but difficult to cure. This happens in affairs of state, for when the evils that arise have been foreseen (which it is only given to a wise man to see), they can be quickly redressed, but when, through not having been foreseen, they have been permitted to grow in a way that every one can see them, there is no longer a remedy. Therefore, the Romans, foreseeing troubles, dealt with them at once, and, even to avoid a war, would not let them come to a head, for they knew that war is not to be avoided, but is only to be put off to the advantage of others; moreover they wished to fight with Philip and Antiochus in Greece so as not to have to do it in Italy; they could have avoided both, but this they did not wish; nor did that ever please them which is for ever in the mouths of the wise ones of our time—let us enjoy the benefits of the time—but rather the benefits of their own valour and prudence, for time drives everything before it, and is able to bring with it good as well as evil, and evil as well as good.

King Louis was brought into Italy by the ambition of the Venetians, who desired to obtain half the state of Lombardy by his intervention. I will not blame the course taken by the king, because, wishing to get a foothold in Italy, and having no friends there—seeing rather that every door was shut to him owing to the conduct of Charles—he was forced to accept those friendships which he could get, and he would have succeeded very quickly in his design if in other matters he had not made some mistakes. The king, however, having acquired Lombardy, regained at once the authority which Charles had lost: Genoa yielded; the Florentines became his friends; the Marquess of Mantua, the Duke of Ferrara, the Bentivogli, my lady of Forli, the Lords of Faenza, of Pesaro, of Rimini, of Camerino, of Piombino, the Lucchese, the Pisans, the Sienese—everybody made advances to him to become his friend. Then could the Venetians realize the rashness of the course taken by them, which, in order that they might secure two towns in Lombardy, had made the king master of two-thirds of Italy.

Let any one now consider that with little difficulty the king could have maintained his position in Italy had he observed the rules laid down above, and kept all his friends secure and protected; for although they were numerous they were both weak and timid, some afraid of the Church, some of the Venetians, and thus they would always have been forced to stand in with him, and by their means he could easily have made himself secure against those who remained powerful. But he was no sooner in Milan than he did the contrary by assisting Pope Alexander to occupy the Romagna. It never occurred to him that by this action he was weakening himself, depriving himself of friends and of those who had thrown themselves into his lap, whilst he aggrandized the Church by adding much temporal power to the spiritual, thus giving it greater authority. And having committed this prime error, he was obliged to follow it up, so much so that, to put an end to the ambition of Alexander, and to prevent his becoming the master of Tuscany, he was himself forced to come into Italy.

And as if it were not enough to have aggrandized the Church, and deprived himself of friends, he, wishing to have the kingdom of Naples, divides it with the King of Spain, and where he was the prime arbiter in Italy he takes an associate, so that the ambitious of that country and the malcontents of his own should have somewhere to shelter; and whereas he could have left in the kingdom his own pensioner as king, he drove him out, to put one there who was able to drive him, Louis, out in turn.

The wish to acquire is in truth very natural and common, and men always do so when they can, and for this they will be praised not blamed; but when they cannot do so, yet wish to do so by any means, then there is folly and blame. Therefore, if France could have attacked Naples with her own forces she ought to have done so; if she could not, then she ought not to have divided it. And if the partition which she made with the Venetians in Lombardy was justified by the excuse that by it she got a foothold in Italy, this other partition merited blame, for it had not the excuse of that necessity.

Therefore Louis made these five errors: he destroyed the minor powers, he increased the strength of one of the greater powers in Italy, he brought in a foreign power, he did not settle in the country, he did not send colonies. Which errors, had he lived, were not enough to injure him had he not made a sixth by taking away their dominions from the Venetians; because, had

he not aggrandized the Church, nor brought
Spain into Italy, it would have been very
reasonable and necessary to humble them; but
having first taken these steps, he ought never to
have consented to their ruin, for they, being
powerful, would always have kept off others
from designs on Lombardy, to which the
Venetians would never have consented except to
become masters themselves there; also because
the others would not wish to take Lombardy
from France in order to give it to the Venetians,
and to run counter to both they would not have
had the courage.

And if any one should say: "King Louis
yielded the Romagna to Alexander and the
kingdom to Spain to avoid war, I answer for the
reasons given above that a blunder ought never
to be perpetrated to avoid war, because it is not
to be avoided, but is only deferred to your
disadvantage. And if another should allege the
pledge which the king had given to the Pope that
he would assist him in the enterprise, in
exchange for the dissolution of his marriage and
for the cap to Rouen, to that I reply what I shall
write later on concerning the faith of princes, and
how it ought to be kept.

Thus King Louis lost Lombardy by not having
followed any of the conditions observed by those

who have taken possession of countries and wished to retain them. Nor is there any miracle in this, but much that is reasonable and quite natural. And on these matters I spoke at Nantes with Rouen, when Valentino, as Cesare Borgia, the son of Pope Alexander, was usually called, occupied the Romagna, and on Cardinal Rouen observing to me that the Italians did not understand war, I replied to him that the French did not understand statecraft, meaning that otherwise they would not have allowed the Church to reach such greatness. And in fact it has been seen that the greatness of the Church and of Spain in Italy has been caused by France, and her ruin may be attributed to them. From this a general rule is drawn which never or rarely fails: that he who is the cause of another becoming powerful is ruined; because that predominancy has been brought about either by astuteness or else by force, and both are distrusted by him who has been raised to power.

CHAPTER 4

Why the Kingdom of Darius, Conquered by Alexander, Did Not Rebel Against the Successors of Alexander at His Death

Considering the difficulties which men have had to hold to a newly acquired state, some might wonder how, seeing that Alexander the Great became the master of Asia in a few years, and died whilst it was scarcely settled (whence it might appear reasonable that the whole empire would have rebelled), nevertheless his successors maintained themselves, and had to meet no other difficulty than that which arose among themselves from their own ambitions.

I answer that the principalities of which one has record are found to be governed in two different ways; either by a prince, with a body of servants, who assist him to govern the kingdom as ministers by his favor and permission; or by a prince and barons, who hold that dignity by antiquity of blood and not by the grace of the prince. Such barons have states and their own subjects, who recognize them as lords and hold them in natural affection. Those states that are governed by a prince and his servants hold their prince in more consideration, because in all the country there is no one who is recognized as superior to him, and if they yield obedience to another they do it as to a minister and official, and they do not bear him any particular affection.

The examples of these two governments in our time are the Turk and the King of France. The entire monarchy of the Turk is governed by one lord, the others are his servants; and, dividing his kingdom into sanjaks (sub-provinces), he sends there different administrators, and shifts and changes them as he chooses. But the King of France is placed in the midst of an ancient body of lords, acknowledged by their own subjects, and beloved by them; they have their own prerogatives, nor can the king take these away except at his peril. Therefore, he who considers both of these states will recognize great difficulties in seizing the state of the Turk, but, once it is conquered, great ease in holding it. The causes of the difficulties in seizing the kingdom of the Turk are that the usurper cannot be called in by the princes of the kingdom, nor can he hope to be assisted in his designs by the revolt of those whom the lord has around him. This arises from the reasons given above; for his ministers, being all slaves and bondmen, can only be corrupted with great difficulty, and one can expect little advantage from them when they have been corrupted, as they cannot carry the people with them, for the reasons assigned. Hence, he who attacks the Turk must bear in mind that he will find him united, and he will have to rely more on his own strength than on the revolt of others; but, if once the Turk has been conquered, and routed in the field in such a way that he cannot replace his armies, there is nothing to fear but the family of this prince, and, this being exterminated, there remains no one to fear, the others having no credit with the people; and as the conqueror did not rely on them before his victory, so he ought not to fear them after it.

The contrary happens in kingdoms governed like that of France, because one can easily enter there by gaining over some baron of the kingdom, for one always finds malcontents and such as desire a change. Such men, for the reasons given, can open the way into the state and render the victory easy; but if you wish to hold it afterwards, you meet with infinite difficulties, both from those who have assisted you and from those you have crushed. Nor is it enough for you to have exterminated the family of the prince, because the lords that remain make themselves the heads of fresh movements against you, and as you are unable either to satisfy or exterminate them, that state is lost whenever time brings the opportunity.

Now if you will consider what was the nature of the government of Darius, you will find it similar to the kingdom of the Turk, and therefore it was only necessary for Alexander, first to overthrow him in the field, and then to take the country from him. After which victory, Darius being killed, the state remained secure to Alexander, for the above reasons. And if his successors had been united they would have enjoyed it securely and at their ease, for there were no tumults raised in the kingdom except those they provoked themselves. But it is impossible to hold with such tranquillity states constituted like that of France. Hence arose those frequent rebellions against the Romans in Spain, France, and Greece, owing to the many principalities there were in these states, of which, as long as the memory of them endured, the Romans always held an insecure possession; but with the power and long continuance of the empire the memory of them passed away, and the Romans then became secure possessors. And when fighting afterwards amongst themselves, each one was able to attach to himself his own parts of the country, according to the authority he had assumed there; and the family of the former lord being exterminated, none other than the Romans were acknowledged.

When these things are remembered no one will marvel at the ease with which Alexander held the Empire of Asia, or at the difficulties which others have had to keep an acquisition, such as Pyrrhus and many more; this is not occasioned by the little or abundance of ability in the conqueror, but by the want of uniformity in the subject state.

CHAPTER 5

Concerning the Way to Govern Cities or Principalities Which Lived Under Their Own Laws Before They Were Annexed

Whenever those states which have been acquired as stated have been accustomed to live under their own laws and in freedom, there are three courses for those who wish to hold them: the first is to ruin them, the next is to reside there in person, the third is to permit them to live under their own laws, drawing a tribute, and establishing within it an oligarchy which will keep it friendly to you. Because such a government, being created by the prince, knows that it cannot stand without his friendship and interest, and does it utmost to support him; and therefore he who would keep a city accustomed to freedom will hold it more easily by the means of its own citizens than in any other way.

There are, for example, the Spartans and the Romans. The Spartans held Athens and Thebes, establishing there an oligarchy, nevertheless they lost them. The Romans, in order to hold Capua, Carthage, and Numantia, dismantled them, and did not lose them. They wished to hold Greece as the Spartans held it, making it free and permitting its laws, and did not succeed. So to hold it they were compelled to dismantle many cities in the country, for in truth there is no safe way to retain them otherwise than by ruining them. And he who becomes master of a city accustomed to freedom and does not destroy it, may expect to be destroyed by it, for in rebellion it has always the watchword of liberty and its ancient privileges as a rallying point, which neither time nor benefits will ever cause it to forget. And whatever you may do or provide against, they never forget that name or their privileges unless they are disunited or dispersed, but at every chance they immediately rally to them, as did Pisa after the hundred years she had been held in bondage by the Florentines.

But when cities or countries are accustomed to live under a prince, and his family is exterminated, they, being on the one hand accustomed to obey and on the other hand not having the old prince, cannot agree in making one from amongst themselves, and they do not know how to govern themselves. For this reason they are very slow to take up arms, and a prince can gain them to himself and secure them much more easily. But in republics there is more vitality, greater hatred, and more desire for vengeance, which will never permit them to allow the memory of their former liberty to rest; so that the safest way is to destroy them or to reside there.

CHAPTER 6

Concerning New Principalities Which Are Acquired by One's Own Arms and Ability

Let no one be surprised if, in speaking of entirely new principalities as I shall do, I adduce the highest examples both of prince and of state; because men, walking almost always in paths beaten by others, and following by imitation their deeds, are yet unable to keep entirely to the ways of others or attain to the power of those they imitate. A wise man ought always to follow the paths beaten by great men, and to imitate those who have been supreme, so that if his ability does not equal theirs, at least it will savor of it. Let him act like the clever archers who, designing to hit the mark which yet appears too far distant, and knowing the limits to which the strength of their bow attains, take aim much higher than the mark, not to reach by their strength or arrow to so great a height, but to be able with the aid of so high an aim to hit the mark they wish to reach.

I say, therefore, that in entirely new principalities, where there is a new prince, more or less difficulty is found in keeping them, accordingly as there is more or less ability in him who has acquired the state. Now, as the fact of becoming a prince from a private station presupposes either ability or fortune, it is clear that one or other of these things will mitigate in some degree many difficulties. Nevertheless, he who has relied least on fortune is established the strongest. Further, it facilitates matters when the prince, having no other state, is compelled to reside there in person.

But to come to those who, by their own ability and not through fortune, have risen to be princes, I say that Moses, Cyrus, Romulus, Theseus, and such like are the most excellent examples. And although one may not discuss Moses, he having been a mere executor of the will of God, yet he ought to be admired, if only for that favor which made him worthy to speak with God. But in considering Cyrus and others who have acquired or founded kingdoms, all will be found admirable; and if their particular deeds and conduct shall be considered, they will not be found inferior to those of Moses, although he had so great a preceptor. And in examining their actions and lives one cannot see that they owed anything to fortune beyond opportunity, which brought them the material to mould into the form which seemed best to them. Without that opportunity their powers of mind would have been extinguished, and without those powers the opportunity would have come in vain.

It was necessary, therefore, to Moses that he should find the people of Israel in Egypt enslaved and oppressed by the Egyptians, in order that they should be disposed to follow him so as to be delivered out of bondage. It was necessary that Romulus should not remain in Alba, and that he should be abandoned at his birth, in order that he should become King of Rome and founder of the fatherland. It was necessary that Cyrus should find the Persians discontented with the government of the Medes, and the Medes soft and effeminate through their long peace. Theseus could not have shown his ability had he not found the Athenians dispersed. These opportunities, therefore, made those men fortunate, and their high ability enabled them to recognize the opportunity whereby their country was ennobled and made famous. Those who by valorous ways become princes, like these men, acquire a principality with difficulty, but they keep it with ease. The difficulties they have in acquiring it rise in part from the new rules and methods which they are forced to introduce to establish their government and its security. And it ought to be remembered that there is nothing more difficult to take in hand, more perilous to conduct, or more uncertain in its success, then to take the lead in the introduction of a new order of things. Because the innovator has for enemies all those who have done well under the old conditions, and lukewarm defenders in those who may do well under the new. This coolness arises partly from fear of the opponents, who have the laws on their side, and partly from the incredulity of men, who do not readily believe in new things until they have had a long experience of them. Thus it happens that whenever those who are hostile have the opportunity to attack they do it like partisans, whilst the others defend lukewarmly, in such wise that the prince is endangered along with them. It is necessary, therefore, if we desire to discuss this matter thoroughly, to inquire whether these innovators can rely on themselves or have to depend on others: that is to say, whether, to consummate their enterprise, have they to use prayers or can they use force? In the first instance they always succeed badly, and never compass anything; but when they can rely on themselves and use force, then they are rarely endangered. Hence it is that all armed prophets have conquered, and the unarmed ones have been destroyed. Besides the reasons mentioned, the nature of the people is variable, and whilst it is easy to persuade them, it is difficult to fix them in that persuasion. And thus it is necessary to take such measures that, when they believe no longer, it may be possible to make them believe by force. If Moses, Cyrus, Theseus, and Romulus had been unarmed they could not have enforced their constitutions for long—as happened in our time to Fra Girolamo Savonarola, who was ruined with his new order of things immediately the multitude believed in him no longer, and he had no means of keeping steadfast those who believed or of making the unbelievers to believe. Therefore such as these have great difficulties in consummating their enterprise, for all their dangers are in the ascent, yet with ability they will overcome them; but when these are overcome, and those who envied them their success are exterminated, they will begin to be respected, and they will continue afterwards powerful, secure, honored, and happy. To these great examples I wish to add a lesser one; still it bears some resemblance to them, and I wish it to suffice me for all of a like kind: it is Hiero the Syracusan. This man rose from a private station to be Prince of Syracuse, nor did he, either, owe anything to fortune but opportunity; for the Syracusans, being oppressed, chose him for their captain; afterwards he was rewarded by being made their prince. He was of so great ability, even as a private citizen, that one who writes of him says he wanted nothing but a kingdom to be a king. This man abolished the old soldiery, organized the new, gave up old alliances, made new ones; and as he had his own soldiers and allies, on such foundations he was able to build any edifice: thus, whilst he had endured much trouble in acquiring, he had but little in keeping.

CHAPTER 7

Concerning New Principalities Which Are Acquired Either by the Arms of Others or by Good Fortune

Those who solely by good fortune become princes from being private citizens have little trouble in rising, but much in keeping atop; they have not any difficulties on the way up, because they fly, but they have many when they reach the summit. Such are those to whom some state is given either for money or by the favor of him who bestows it; as happened to many in Greece, in the cities of Ionia and of the Hellespont, where princes were made by Darius, in order that they might hold the cities both for his security and his glory; as also were those emperors who, by the corruption of the soldiers, from being citizens came to empire. Such stand simply elevated upon the goodwill and the fortune of him who has elevated them—two most inconstant and unstable things. Neither have they the knowledge requisite for the position; because, unless they are men of great worth and ability, it is not reasonable to expect that they should know how to command, having always lived in a private condition; besides, they cannot hold it because they have not forces which they can keep friendly and faithful.

States that rise unexpectedly, then, like all other things in nature which are born and grow rapidly, cannot leave their foundations and correspondencies fixed in such a way that the first storm will not overthrow them; unless, as is said, those who unexpectedly become princes are men of so much ability that they know they have to be prepared at once to hold that which fortune has thrown into their laps, and that those foundations, which others have laid before they became princes, they must lay afterwards.

Concerning these two methods of rising to be a prince by ability or fortune, I wish to adduce two examples within our own recollection, and these are Francesco Sforza and Cesare Borgia. Francesco, by proper means and with great ability, from being a private person rose to be Duke of Milan, and that which he had acquired with a thousand anxieties he kept with little trouble. On the other hand, Cesare Borgia, called by the people Duke Valentino, acquired his state during the ascendancy of his father, and on its decline he lost it, notwithstanding that he had taken every measure and done all that ought to be done by a wise and able man to fix firmly his roots in the states which the arms and fortunes of others had bestowed on him. Because, as is stated above, he who has not first laid his foundations may be able with great ability to lay them afterwards, but they will be laid with trouble to the architect and danger to the building. If, therefore, all the steps taken by the duke be considered, it will be seen that he laid solid foundations for his future power, and I do not consider it superfluous to discuss them, because I do not know what better precepts to give a new prince than the example of his actions; and if his dispositions were of no avail, that was not his fault, but the extraordinary and extreme malignity of fortune.

Alexander the Sixth, in wishing to aggrandize the duke, his son, had many immediate and prospective difficulties. Firstly, he did not see his way to make him master of any state that was not a state of the Church; and if he was willing to rob the Church he knew that the Duke of Milan and the Venetians would not consent, because Faenza and Rimini were already under the protection of the Venetians. Besides this, he saw the arms of Italy, especially those by which he might have been assisted, in hands that would fear the aggrandizement of the Pope, namely, the Orsini and the Colonnesi and their following. It behooved him, therefore, to upset this state of affairs and embroil the powers, so as to make himself securely master of part of their states. This was easy for him to do, because he found the Venetians, moved by other reasons, inclined to bring back the French into Italy; he would not only not oppose this, but he would render it more easy by dissolving the former marriage of King Louis. Therefore the king came into Italy with the assistance of the Venetians and the consent of Alexander. He was no sooner in Milan than the Pope had soldiers from him for the attempt on the Romagna, which yielded to him on the reputation of the king. The duke, therefore, having acquired the Romagna and beaten the Colonnesi, while wishing to hold that and to advance further, was hindered by two things: the one, his forces did not appear loyal to him, the other, the goodwill of France: that is to say, he feared that the forces of the Orsini, which he was using, would not stand to him, that not only might they hinder him from winning more, but might themselves seize what he had won,

and that the king might also do the same. Of the
Orsini he had a warning when, after taking
Faenza and attacking Bologna, he saw them go
very unwillingly to that attack. And as to the
king, he learned his mind when he himself, after
taking the Duchy of Urbino, attacked Tuscany,
and the king made him desist from that
undertaking; hence the duke decided to depend
no more upon the arms and the luck of others.
For the first thing he weakened the Orsini and
Colonnesi parties in Rome, by gaining to himself
all their adherents who were gentlemen, making
them his gentlemen, giving them good pay, and,
according to their rank, honoring them with
office and command in such a way that in a few
months all attachment to the factions was
destroyed and turned entirely to the duke. After
this he awaited an opportunity to crush the
Orsini, having scattered the adherents of the
Colonna house. This came to him soon and he
used it well; for the Orsini, perceiving at length
that the aggrandizement of the duke and the
Church was ruin to them, called a meeting of the
Magione in Perugia. From this sprung the
rebellion at Urbino and the tumults in the
Romagna, with endless dangers to the duke, all
of which he overcame with the help of the
French. Having restored his authority, not to

leave it at risk by trusting either to the French or other outside forces, he had recourse to his wiles, and he knew so well how to conceal his mind that, by the mediation of Signor Pagolo—whom the duke did not fail to secure with all kinds of attention, giving him money, apparel, and horses—the Orsini were reconciled, so that their simplicity brought them into his power at Sinigalia. Having exterminated the leaders, and turned their partisans into his friends, the duke laid sufficiently good foundations to his power, having all the Romagna and the Duchy of Urbino; and the people now beginning to appreciate their prosperity, he gained them all over to himself. And as this point is worthy of notice, and to be imitated by others, I am not willing to leave it out.

When the duke occupied the Romagna he found it under the rule of weak masters, who rather plundered their subjects than ruled them, and gave them more cause for disunion than for union, so that the country was full of robbery, quarrels, and every kind of violence; and so, wishing to bring back peace and obedience to authority, he considered it necessary to give it a good governor. Thereupon he promoted Messer Ramiro d'Orco, a swift and cruel man, to whom he gave the fullest power. This man in a short

time restored peace and unity with the greatest
success. Afterwards the duke considered that it
was not advisable to confer such excessive
authority, for he had no doubt but that he would
become odious, so he set up a court of judgment
in the country, under a most excellent president,
wherein all cities had their advocates. And
because he knew that the past severity had
caused some hatred against himself, so, to clear
himself in the minds of the people, and gain
them entirely to himself, he desired to show that,
if any cruelty had been practiced, it had not
originated with him, but in the natural sternness
of the minister. Under this pretense he took
Ramiro, and one morning caused him to be
executed and left on the piazza at Cesena with
the block and a bloody knife at his side. The
barbarity of this spectacle caused the people to be
at once satisfied and dismayed.

But let us return whence we started. I say that
the duke, finding himself now sufficiently
powerful and partly secured from immediate
dangers by having armed himself in his own
way, and having in a great measure crushed
those forces in his vicinity that could injure him if
he wished to proceed with his conquest, had next
to consider France, for he knew that the king,
who too late was aware of his mistake, would not

support him. And from this time he began to
seek new alliances and to temporize with France
in the expedition which she was making towards
the kingdom of Naples against the Spaniards
who were besieging Gaeta. It was his intention to
secure himself against them, and this he would
have quickly accomplished had Alexander lived.
Such was his line of action as to present affairs.
But as to the future he had to fear, in the first
place, that a new successor to the Church might
not be friendly to him and might seek to take
from him that which Alexander had given him,
so he decided to act in four ways. Firstly, by
exterminating the families of those lords whom
he had despoiled, so as to take away that pretext
from the Pope. Secondly, by winning to himself
all the gentlemen of Rome, so as to be able to
curb the Pope with their aid, as has been
observed. Thirdly, by converting the college more
to himself. Fourthly, by acquiring so much power
before the Pope should die that he could by his
own measures resist the first shock. Of these four
things, at the death of Alexander, he had
accomplished three. For he had killed as many of
the dispossessed lords as he could lay hands on,
and few had escaped; he had won over the
Roman gentlemen, and he had the most
numerous party in the college. And as to any

fresh acquisition, he intended to become master of Tuscany, for he already possessed Perugia and Piombino, and Pisa was under his protection. And as he had no longer to study France (for the French were already driven out of the kingdom of Naples by the Spaniards, and in this way both were compelled to buy his goodwill), he pounced down upon Pisa. After this, Lucca and Siena yielded at once, partly through hatred and partly through fear of the Florentines; and the Florentines would have had no remedy had he continued to prosper, as he was prospering the year that Alexander died, for he had acquired so much power and reputation that he would have stood by himself, and no longer have depended on the luck and the forces of others, but solely on his own power and ability.

But Alexander died five years after he had first drawn the sword. He left the duke with the state of Romagna alone consolidated, with the rest in the air, between two most powerful hostile armies, and sick unto death. Yet there was in the duke such boldness and ability, and he knew so well how men are to be won or lost, and so firm were the foundations which in so short a time he had laid, that if he had not had those armies on his back, or if he had been in good health, he would have overcome all difficulties. And it is seen that his foundations were good, for the Romagna awaited him for more than a month. In Rome, although but half alive, he remained secure; and whilst the Baglioni, the Vitelli, and the Orsini might come to Rome, they could not effect anything against him. If he could not have made Pope him whom he wished, at least the one whom he did not wish would not have been elected. But if he had been in sound health at the death of Alexander, everything would have been different to him. On the day that Julius the Second was elected, he told me that he had thought of everything that might occur at the death of his father, and had provided a remedy for all, except that he had never anticipated that, when the death did happen, he himself would be on the point to die.

When all the actions of the duke are recalled, I do not know how to blame him, but rather it appears to be, as I have said, that I ought to offer him for imitation to all those who, by the fortune or the arms of others, are raised to government. Because he, having a lofty spirit and far-reaching aims, could not have regulated his conduct otherwise, and only the shortness of the life of Alexander and his own sickness frustrated his designs. Therefore, he who considers it necessary to secure himself in his new principality, to win friends, to overcome either by force or fraud, to make himself beloved and feared by the people, to be followed and revered by the soldiers, to exterminate those who have power or reason to hurt him, to change the old order of things for new, to be severe and gracious, magnanimous and liberal, to destroy a disloyal soldiery and to create new, to maintain friendship with kings and princes in such a way that they must help him with zeal and offend with caution, cannot find a more lively example than the actions of this man.

Only can he be blamed for the election of Julius the Second, in whom he made a bad choice, because, as is said, not being able to elect a Pope to his own mind, he could have hindered any other from being elected Pope; and he ought never to have consented to the election of any cardinal whom he had injured or who had cause to fear him if they became pontiff. For men injure either from fear or hatred. Those whom he had injured, amongst others, were San Pietro ad Vincula, Colonna, San Giorgio, and Ascanio. The rest, in becoming Pope, had to fear him, Rouen and the Spaniards excepted; the latter from their relationship and obligations, the former from his influence, the kingdom of France having relations with him. Therefore, above everything, the duke ought to have created a Spaniard Pope, and, failing him, he ought to have consented to Rouen and not San Pietro da Vincula. He who believes that new benefits will cause great personages to forget old injuries is deceived. Therefore, the duke erred in his choice, and it was the cause of his ultimate ruin.

CHAPTER 8

Concerning Those Who Have Obtained a Principality by Wickedness

Although a prince may rise from a private station in two ways, neither of which can be entirely attributed to fortune or genius, yet it is manifest to me that I must not be silent on them, although one could be more copiously treated when I discuss republics. These methods are when, either by some wicked or nefarious ways, one ascends to the principality, or when by the favor of his fellow citizens a private person becomes the prince of his country. And speaking of the first method, it will be illustrated by two examples—one ancient, the other modern—and without entering further into the subject, I consider these two examples will suffice those who may be compelled to follow them.

Agathocles, the Sicilian, became King of Syracuse not only from a private but from a low and abject position. This man, the son of a potter, through all the changes in his fortunes always led an infamous life. Nevertheless, he accompanied his infamies with so much ability of mind and body that, having devoted himself to the military profession, he rose through its ranks to be Praetor of Syracuse. Being established in that position, and having deliberately resolved to make himself prince and to seize by violence, without obligation to others, that which had been conceded to him by assent, he came to an understanding for this purpose with Amilcar, the Carthaginian, who, with his army, was fighting in Sicily. One morning he assembled the people and the senate of Syracuse, as if he had to discuss with them things relating to the Republic, and at a given signal the soldiers killed all the senators and the richest of the people; these dead, he seized and held the princedom of that city without any civil commotion. And although he was twice routed by the Carthaginians, and ultimately besieged, yet not only was he able to defend his city, but leaving part of his men for its defense, with the others he attacked Africa, and in a short time raised the siege of Syracuse. The Carthaginians, reduced to extreme necessity, were compelled to come to terms with Agathocles, and, leaving Sicily to him, had to be content with the possession of Africa.

Therefore, he who considers the actions and the genius of this man will see nothing, or little, which can be attributed to fortune, inasmuch as he attained pre-eminence, as is shown above, not by the favor of any one, but step by step in the military profession, which steps were gained with a thousand troubles and perils, and were afterwards boldly held by him with many hazardous dangers. Yet it cannot be called talent to slay fellow citizens, to deceive friends, to be without faith, without mercy, without religion; such methods may gain empire, but not glory. Still, if the courage of Agathocles in entering into and extricating himself from dangers be considered, together with his greatness of mind in enduring and overcoming hardships, it cannot be seen why he should be esteemed less than the most notable captain. Nevertheless, his barbarous cruelty and inhumanity with infinite wickedness do not permit him to be celebrated among the most excellent men. What he achieved cannot be attributed either to fortune or genius.

In our times, during the rule of Alexander the Sixth, Oliverotto da Fermo, having been left an orphan many years before, was brought up by his maternal uncle, Giovanni Fogliani, and in the early days of his youth sent to fight under

Pagolo Vitelli, that, being trained under his discipline, he might attain some high position in the military profession. After Pagolo died, he fought under his brother Vitellozzo, and in a very short time, being endowed with wit and a vigorous body and mind, he became the first man in his profession. But it appearing a paltry thing to serve under others, he resolved, with the aid of some citizens of Fermo, to whom the slavery of their country was dearer than its liberty, and with the help of the Vitelleschi, to seize Fermo. So he wrote to Giovanni Fogliani that, having been away from home for many years, he wished to visit him and his city, and in some measure to look upon his patrimony; and although he had not labored to acquire anything except honor, yet, in order that the citizens should see he had not spent his time in vain, he desired to come honorably, so would be accompanied by one hundred horsemen, his friends and retainers; and he entreated Giovanni to arrange that he should be received honorably by the Fermians, all of which would be not only to his honor, but also to that of Giovanni himself, who had brought him up.

Giovanni, therefore, did not fail in any attentions due to his nephew, and he caused him to be honorably received by the Fermians, and he

lodged him in his own house, where, having
passed some days, and having arranged what
was necessary for his wicked designs, Oliverotto
gave a solemn banquet to which he invited
Giovanni Fogliani and the chiefs of Fermo. When
the viands and all the other entertainments that
are usual in such banquets were finished,
Oliverotto artfully began certain grave
discourses, speaking of the greatness of Pope
Alexander and his son Cesare, and of their
enterprises, to which discourse Giovanni and
others answered; but he rose at once, saying that
such matters ought to be discussed in a more
private place, and he betook himself to a
chamber, whither Giovanni and the rest of the
citizens went in after him. No sooner were they
seated than soldiers issued from secret places and
slaughtered Giovanni and the rest. After these
murders Oliverotto, mounted on horseback, rode
up and down the town and besieged the chief
magistrate in the palace, so that in fear the people
were forced to obey him, and to form a
government, of which he made himself the
prince. He killed all the malcontents who were
able to injure him, and strengthened himself with
new civil and military ordinances, in such a way
that, in the year during which he held the
principality, not only was he secure in the city of

Fermo, but he had become formidable to all his neighbors. And his destruction would have been as difficult as that of Agathocles if he had not allowed himself to be overreached by Cesare Borgia, who took him with the Orsini and Vitelli at Sinigalia, as was stated above. Thus one year after he had committed this parricide, he was strangled, together with Vitellozzo, whom he had made his leader in valour and wickedness. Some may wonder how it can happen that Agathocles, and his like, after infinite treacheries and cruelties, should live for long secure in his country, and defend himself from external enemies, and never be conspired against by his own citizens; seeing that many others, by means of cruelty, have never been able even in peaceful times to hold the state, still less in the doubtful times of war. I believe that this follows from severities being badly or properly used. Those may be called properly used, if of evil it is possible to speak well, that are applied at one blow and are necessary to one's security, and that are not persisted in afterwards unless they can be turned to the advantage of the subjects. The badly employed are those which, notwithstanding they may be few in the commencement, multiply with time rather than decrease. Those who practice the first system are able, by aid of God or man, to mitigate in some degree their rule, as Agathocles did. It is impossible for those who follow the other to maintain themselves.

Hence it is to be remarked that, in seizing a state, the usurper ought to examine closely all those injuries which it is necessary for him to inflict, and to do them all at one stroke so as not to have to repeat them daily; and thus by not unsettling men he will be able to reassure them, and win them to himself by benefits. He who does otherwise, either from timidity or evil advice, is always compelled to keep the knife in his hand; neither can he rely on his subjects, nor can they attach themselves to him, owing to their continued and repeated wrongs. For injuries ought to be done all at one time, so that, being tasted less, they offend less; benefits ought to be given little by little, so that the flavor of them may last longer. And above all things, a prince ought to live amongst his people in such a way that no unexpected circumstances, whether of good or evil, shall make him change; because if the necessity for this comes in troubled times, you are too late for harsh measures; and mild ones will not help you, for they will be considered as forced from you, and no one will be under any obligation to you for them.

CHAPTER 9

Concerning a Civil Principality

But coming to the other point—where a leading citizen becomes the prince of his country, not by wickedness or any intolerable violence, but by the favor of his fellow citizens—this may be called a civil principality: nor is genius or fortune altogether necessary to attain to it, but rather a happy shrewdness. I say then that such a principality is obtained either by the favor of the people or by the favor of the nobles. Because in all cities these two distinct parties are found, and from this it arises that the people do not wish to be ruled nor oppressed by the nobles, and the nobles wish to rule and oppress the people; and from these two opposite desires there arises in cities one of three results, either a principality, self government, or anarchy.

A principality is created either by the people or by the nobles, accordingly as one or other of them has the opportunity; for the nobles, seeing they cannot withstand the people, begin to cry up the reputation of one of themselves, and they make him a prince, so that under his shadow they can give vent to their ambitions. The people, finding they cannot resist the nobles, also cry up the reputation of one of themselves, and make him a prince so as to be defended by his authority. He who obtains sovereignty by the assistance of the nobles maintains himself with more difficulty than he who comes to it by the aid of the people, because the former finds himself with many around him who consider themselves his equals, and because of this he can neither rule nor manage them to his liking. But he who reaches sovereignty by popular favor finds himself alone, and has none around him, or few, who are not prepared to obey him.

Besides this, one cannot by fair dealing, and without injury to others, satisfy the nobles, but you can satisfy the people, for their object is more righteous than that of the nobles, the latter wishing to oppress, while the former only desire not to be oppressed. It is to be added also that a prince can never secure himself against a hostile people, because of their being too many, whilst from the nobles he can secure himself, as they are few in number. The worst that a prince may expect from a hostile people is to be abandoned by them; but from hostile nobles he has not only

to fear abandonment, but also that they will rise
against him; for they, being in these affairs more
far-seeing and astute, always come forward in
time to save themselves, and to obtain favors
from him whom they expect to prevail. Further,
the prince is compelled to live always with the
same people, but he can do well without the
same nobles, being able to make and unmake
them daily, and to give or take away authority
when it pleases him. Therefore, to make this
point clearer, I say that the nobles ought to be
looked at mainly in two ways: that is to say, they
either shape their course in such a way as binds
them entirely to your fortune, or they do not.
Those who so bind themselves, and are not
rapacious, ought to be honored and loved; those
who do not bind themselves may be dealt with in
two ways; they may fail to do this through
pusillanimity and a natural want of courage, in
which case you ought to make use of them,
especially of those who are of good counsel; and
thus, whilst in prosperity you honor them, in
adversity you do not have to fear them. But
when for their own ambitious ends they shun
binding themselves, it is a token that they are
giving more thought to themselves than to you,
and a prince ought to guard against such, and to
fear them as if they were open enemies, because

in adversity they always help to ruin him.

Therefore, one who becomes a prince through the favor of the people ought to keep them friendly, and this he can easily do seeing they only ask not to be oppressed by him. But one who, in opposition to the people, becomes a prince by the favor of the nobles, ought, above everything, to seek to win the people over to himself, and this he may easily do if he takes them under his protection. Because men, when they receive good from him of whom they were expecting evil, are bound more closely to their benefactor; thus the people quickly become more devoted to him than if he had been raised to the principality by their favors; and the prince can win their affections in many ways, but as these vary according to the circumstances, one cannot give fixed rules, so I omit them; but, I repeat, it is necessary for a prince to have the people friendly, otherwise he has no security in adversity. Nabis, Prince of the Spartans, sustained the attack of all Greece, and of a victorious Roman army, and against them he defended his country and his government; and for the overcoming of this peril it was only necessary for him to make himself secure against a few, but this would not have been sufficient had the people been hostile. And do not let any one impugn this statement with the trite proverb that "He who builds on the people, builds on the mud," for this is true when a private citizen makes a foundation there, and persuades himself that the people will free him when he is oppressed by his enemies or by the magistrates; wherein he would find himself very often deceived, as happened to the Gracchi in Rome and to Messer Giorgio Scal in Florence. But granted a prince who has established himself as above, who can command, and is a man of courage, undismayed in adversity, who does not fail in other qualifications, and who, by his resolution and energy, keeps the whole people encouraged—such a one will never find himself deceived in them, and it will be shown that he has laid his foundations well.

These principalities are liable to danger when they are passing from the civil to the absolute order of government, for such princes either rule personally or through magistrates. In the latter case their government is weaker and more insecure, because it rests entirely on the goodwill of those citizens who are raised to the magistracy, and who, especially in troubled times, can destroy the government with great ease, either by intrigue or open defiance; and the prince has not the chance amid tumults to exercise absolute authority, because the citizens and subjects, accustomed to receive orders from magistrates, are not of a mind to obey him amid these confusions, and there will always be in doubtful times a scarcity of men whom he can trust. For such a prince cannot rely upon what he observes in quiet times, when citizens have need of the state, because then every one agrees with him; they all promise, and when death is far distant they all wish to die for him; but in troubled times, when the state has need of its citizens, then he finds but few. And so much the more is this experiment dangerous, inasmuch as it can only be tried once. Therefore a wise prince ought to adopt such a course that his citizens will always in every sort and kind of circumstance have need of the state and of him, and then he will always find them faithful.

CHAPTER 10

Concerning the Way in Which the Strength of All Principalities Ought to Be Measured

It is necessary to consider another point in examining the character of these principalities: that is, whether a prince has such power that, in case of need, he can support himself with his own resources, or whether he has always need of the assistance of others. And to make this quite clear I say that I consider those who are able to support themselves by their own resources who can, either by abundance of men or money, raise a sufficient army to join battle against any one who comes to attack them; and I consider those always to have need of others who cannot show themselves against the enemy in the field, but are forced to defend themselves by sheltering behind walls. The first case has been discussed, but we will speak of it again should it recur. In the second case one can say nothing except to

encourage such princes to provision and fortify
their towns, and not on any account to defend
the country. And whoever shall fortify his town
well, and shall have managed the other concerns
of his subjects in the way stated above, and to be
often repeated, will never be attacked without
great caution, for men are always adverse to
enterprises where difficulties can be seen, and it
will be seen not to be an easy thing to attack one
who has his town well fortified, and is not hated
by his people.

The cities of Germany are absolutely free, they
own but little country around them, and they
yield obedience to the emperor when it suits
them; nor do they fear this or any other power
they may have near them, because they are
fortified in such a way that every one thinks the
taking of them by assault would be tedious and
difficult, seeing they have proper ditches and
walls, they have sufficient artillery, and they
always keep in public depots enough for one
year's eating, drinking, and firing. And beyond
this, to keep the people quiet and without loss to
the state, they always have the means of giving
work to the community in those labors that are
the life and strength of the city, and in the pursuit
of which the people are supported; they also hold
military exercises in repute, and moreover have

many ordinances to uphold them.

Therefore, a prince who has a strong city, and has not made himself odious, will not be attacked, or if any one should attack he will only be driven off with disgrace; again, because the affairs of this world are so changeable, it is almost impossible to keep an army a whole year in the field without being interfered with. And whoever should reply: If the people have property outside the city, and see it burnt, they will not remain patient, and the long siege and self-interest will make them forget their prince; to this I answer that a powerful and courageous prince will overcome all such difficulties by giving at one time hope to his subjects that the evil will not be for long, at another time fear of the cruelty of the enemy, then preserving himself adroitly from those subjects who seem to him to be too bold.

Further, the enemy would naturally on his arrival at once burn and ruin the country at the time when the spirits of the people are still hot and ready for the defense; and, therefore, so much the less ought the prince to hesitate; because after a time, when spirits have cooled, the damage is already done, the ills are incurred, and there is no longer any remedy; and therefore they are so much the more ready to unite with their prince, he appearing to be under obligations to them now that their houses have been burnt and their possessions ruined in his defense. For it is the nature of men to be bound by the benefits they confer as much as by those they receive.

Therefore, if everything is well considered, it will not be difficult for a wise prince to keep the minds of his citizens steadfast from first to last, when he does not fail to support and defend them.

CHAPTER 11

Concerning Ecclesiastical Principalities

It only remains now to speak of ecclesiastical principalities, touching which all difficulties are prior to getting possession, because they are acquired either by capacity or good fortune, and they can be held without either; for they are sustained by the ancient ordinances of religion, which are so all-powerful, and of such a character that the principalities may be held no matter how their princes behave and live. These princes alone have states and do not defend them; and they have subjects and do not rule them; and the states, although unguarded, are not taken from them, and the subjects, although not ruled, do not care, and they have neither the desire nor the ability to alienate themselves. Such principalities only are secure and happy. But being upheld by powers, to which the human mind cannot reach, I shall speak no more of them, because, being exalted and maintained by God, it would be the act of a presumptuous and rash man to discuss them.

Nevertheless, if any one should ask of me how comes it that the Church has attained such greatness in temporal power, seeing that from Alexander backwards the Italian potentates (not only those who have been called potentates, but every baron and lord, though the smallest) have valued the temporal power very slightly—yet now a king of France trembles before it, and it has been able to drive him from Italy, and to ruin the Venetians—although this may be very manifest, it does not appear to me superfluous to recall it in some measure to memory. Before Charles, King of France, passed into Italy, this country was under the dominion of the Pope, the Venetians, the King of Naples, the Duke of Milan, and the Florentines. These potentates had two principal anxieties: the one, that no foreigner should enter Italy under arms; the other, that none of themselves should seize more territory. Those about whom there was the most anxiety were the Pope and the Venetians. To restrain the Venetians the union of all the others was necessary, as it was for the defense of Ferrara; and to keep down the Pope they made use of the barons of Rome, who, being divided into two factions, Orsini and Colonnesi, had always a pretext for disorder, and, standing with arms in their hands under the eyes of the Pontiff, kept the pontificate weak and powerless. And although there might arise sometimes a courageous pope, such as Sixtus, yet neither fortune nor wisdom could rid him of these annoyances. And the short life of a pope is also a cause of weakness; for in the ten years which is the average life of a pope, he can with difficulty lower one of the factions; and if, so to speak, one people should almost destroy the Colonnesi, another would arise hostile to the Orsini, who would support their opponents, and yet would not have time to ruin the Orsini. This was the reason why the temporal powers of the pope were little esteemed in Italy.

Alexander the Sixth arose afterwards, who of all the pontiffs that have ever been showed how a pope with both money and arms was able to prevail; and through the instrumentality of the Duke Valentino, and by reason of the entry of the French, he brought about all those things which I have discussed above in the actions of the duke. And although his intention was not to aggrandize the Church, but the duke, nevertheless, what he did contributed to the greatness of the Church, which, after his death and the ruin of the duke, became the heir to all his labors.

Pope Julius came afterwards and found the Church strong, possessing all the Romagna, the barons of Rome reduced to impotence, and, through the chastisements of Alexander, the factions wiped out; he also found the way open to accumulate money in a manner such as had never been practiced before Alexander's time. Such things Julius not only followed, but improved upon, and he intended to gain Bologna, to ruin the Venetians, and to drive the French out of Italy. All of these enterprises prospered with him, and so much the more to his credit, inasmuch as he did everything to strengthen the Church and not any private person. He kept also the Orsini and Colonnesi factions within the bounds in which he found them; and although there was among them some mind to make disturbance, nevertheless he held two things firm: the one, the greatness of the Church, with which he terrified them; and the other, not allowing them to have their own cardinals, who caused the disorders among them. For whenever these factions have their cardinals they do not remain quiet for long, because cardinals foster the factions in Rome and out of it, and the barons are compelled to support them, and thus from the ambitions of prelates arise disorders and tumults among the barons. For these reasons his Holiness Pope Leo found the pontificate most powerful, and it is to be hoped that, if others made it great in arms, he will make it still greater and more venerated by his goodness and infinite other virtues.

CHAPTER 12

How Many Kinds of Soldiery There Are, and Concerning Mercenaries

Having discoursed particularly on the characteristics of such principalities as in the beginning I proposed to discuss, and having considered in some degree the causes of their being good or bad, and having shown the methods by which many have sought to acquire them and to hold them, it now remains for me to discuss generally the means of offense and defense which belong to each of them.

We have seen above how necessary it is for a prince to have his foundations well laid, otherwise it follows of necessity he will go to ruin. The chief foundations of all states, new as well as old or composite, are good laws and good arms; and as there cannot be good laws where the state is not well armed, it follows that where they are well armed they have good laws. I shall leave the laws out of the discussion and shall speak of the arms.

I say, therefore, that the arms with which a prince defends his state are either his own, or they are mercenaries, auxiliaries, or mixed. Mercenaries and auxiliaries are useless and dangerous; and if one holds his state based on these arms, he will stand neither firm nor safe; for they are disunited, ambitious, and without discipline, unfaithful, valiant before friends, cowardly before enemies; they have neither the fear of God nor fidelity to men, and destruction is deferred only so long as the attack is; for in peace one is robbed by them, and in war by the enemy. The fact is that they have no other attraction or reason for keeping the field than a trifle of stipend, which is not sufficient to make them willing to die for you. They are ready enough to be your soldiers whilst you do not make war, but if war comes they take themselves off or run from the foe; which I should have little trouble to prove, for the ruin of Italy has been caused by nothing else than by resting all her hopes for many years on mercenaries, and although they formerly made some display and appeared valiant amongst themselves, yet when the foreigners came they showed what they were. Thus it was that Charles, King of France, was allowed to seize Italy with chalk in hand; and he who told us that our sins were the cause of it told the truth, but they were not the sins he imagined, but those which I have related. And as they were the sins of princes, it is the princes who have also suffered the penalty.

I wish to demonstrate further the infelicity of these arms. The mercenary captains are either capable men or they are not; if they are, you cannot trust them, because they always aspire to their own greatness, either by oppressing you, who are their master, or others contrary to your intentions; but if the captain is not skillful, you are ruined in the usual way.

And if it be urged that whoever is armed will act in the same way, whether mercenary or not, I reply that when arms have to be resorted to, either by a prince or a republic, then the prince ought to go in person and perform the duty of a captain; the republic has to send its citizens, and when one is sent who does not turn out satisfactorily, it ought to recall him, and when one is worthy, to hold him by the laws so that he does not leave the command. And experience has shown princes and republics, single-handed, making the greatest progress, and mercenaries doing nothing except damage; and it is more difficult to bring a republic, armed with its own arms, under the sway of one of its citizens than it is to bring one armed with foreign arms.

Rome and Sparta stood for many ages armed and free. The Switzers are completely armed and quite free.

Of ancient mercenaries, for example, there are the Carthaginians, who were oppressed by their mercenary soldiers after the first war with the Romans, although the Carthaginians had their own citizens for captains. After the death of Epaminondas, Philip of Macedon was made captain of their soldiers by the Thebans, and after victory he took away their liberty.

Duke Filippo being dead, the Milanese enlisted Francesco Sforza against the Venetians, and he, having overcome the enemy at Caravaggio, allied himself with them to crush the Milanese, his masters. His father, Sforza, having been engaged by Queen Johanna of Naples, left her unprotected, so that she was forced to throw herself into the arms of the King of Aragon, in order to save her kingdom. And if the Venetians and Florentines formerly extended their dominions by these arms, and yet their captains did not make themselves princes, but have defended them, I reply that the Florentines in this case have been favored by chance, for of the able captains, of whom they might have stood in fear, some have not conquered, some have been opposed, and others have turned their ambitions elsewhere. One who did not conquer was Giovanni Acuto, and since he did not conquer his fidelity cannot be proved; but every one will acknowledge that, had he conquered, the Florentines would have stood at his discretion. Sforza had the Bracceschi always against him, so they watched each other. Francesco turned his ambition to Lombardy; Braccio against the Church and the kingdom of Naples. But let us come to that which happened a short while ago.

The Florentines appointed as their captain Pagolo Vitelli, a most prudent man, who from a private position had risen to the greatest renown. If this man had taken Pisa, nobody can deny that it would have been proper for the Florentines to keep in with him, for if he became the soldier of their enemies they had no means of resisting, and if they held to him they must obey him.

The Venetians, if their achievements are considered, will be seen to have acted safely and gloriously so long as they sent to war their own men, when with armed gentlemen and plebians they did valiantly. This was before they turned to enterprises on land, but when they began to fight on land they forsook this virtue and followed the custom of Italy. And in the beginning of their expansion on land, through not having much territory, and because of their great reputation, they had not much to fear from their captains; but when they expanded, as under Carmignuola, they had a taste of this mistake; for, having found him a most valiant man (they beat the Duke of Milan under his leadership), and, on the other hand, knowing how lukewarm he was in the war, they feared they would no longer conquer under him, and for this reason they were not willing, nor were they able, to let him go; and so, not to lose again that which they had acquired, they were compelled, in order to secure themselves, to murder him. They had afterwards for their captains Bartolomeo da Bergamo, Roberto da San Severino, the count of Pitigliano, and the like, under whom they had to dread loss and not gain, as happened afterwards at Vaila, where in one battle they lost that which in eight hundred years they had acquired with so much trouble. Because from such arms conquests come but slowly, long delayed and inconsiderable, but the losses sudden and portentous.

And as with these examples I have reached Italy, which has been ruled for many years by mercenaries, I wish to discuss them more seriously, in order that, having seen their rise and progress, one may be better prepared to counteract them. You must understand that the empire has recently come to be repudiated in

Italy, that the Pope has acquired more temporal power, and that Italy has been divided up into more states, for the reason that many of the great cities took up arms against their nobles, who, formerly favored by the emperor, were oppressing them, whilst the Church was favoring them so as to gain authority in temporal power: in many others their citizens became princes. From this it came to pass that Italy fell partly into the hands of the Church and of republics, and, the Church consisting of priests and the republic of citizens unaccustomed to arms, both commenced to enlist foreigners.

The first who gave renown to this soldiery was Alberigo da Conio, the Romagnian. From the school of this man sprang, among others, Braccio and Sforza, who in their time were the arbiters of Italy. After these came all the other captains who till now have directed the arms of Italy; and the end of all their valour has been, that she has been overrun by Charles, robbed by Louis, ravaged by Ferdinand, and insulted by the Switzers. The principle that has guided them has been, first, to lower the credit of infantry so that they might increase their own. They did this because, subsisting on their pay and without territory, they were unable to support many soldiers, and a few infantry did not give them

any authority; so they were led to employ
cavalry, with a moderate force of which they
were maintained and honored; and affairs were
brought to such a pass that, in an army of twenty
thousand soldiers, there were not to be found
two thousand foot soldiers. They had, besides
this, used every art to lessen fatigue and danger
to themselves and their soldiers, not killing in
the fray, but taking prisoners and liberating
without ransom. They did not attack towns at
night, nor did the garrisons of the towns attack
encampments at night; they did not surround
the camp either with stockade or ditch, nor did
they campaign in the winter. All these things
were permitted by their military rules, and
devised by them to avoid, as I have said, both
fatigue and dangers; thus they have brought
Italy to slavery and contempt.

CHAPTER 13

Concerning Auxiliaries, Mixed Soldiery, and One's Own

Auxiliaries, which are the other useless arm, are employed when a prince is called in with his forces to aid and defend, as was done by Pope Julius in the most recent times; for he, having, in the enterprise against Ferrara, had poor proof of his mercenaries, turned to auxiliaries, and stipulated with Ferdinand, King of Spain, for his assistance with men and arms. These arms may be useful and good in themselves, but for him who calls them in they are always disadvantageous; for losing, one is undone, and winning, one is their captive.

And although ancient histories may be full of examples, I do not wish to leave this recent one of Pope Julius the Second, the peril of which cannot fail to be perceived; for he, wishing to get Ferrara, threw himself entirely into the hands of the foreigner. But his good fortune brought about a third event, so that he did not reap the fruit of his rash choice; because, having his auxiliaries routed at Ravenna, and the Switzers having risen and driven out the conquerors (against all expectation, both his and others), it so came to pass that he did not become prisoner to his enemies, they having fled, nor to his auxiliaries, he having conquered by other arms than theirs.

The Florentines, being entirely without arms, sent ten thousand Frenchmen to take Pisa, whereby they ran into more danger than at any other time of their troubles.

The Emperor of Constantinople, to oppose his neighbors, sent ten thousand Turks into Greece, who, on the war being finished, were not willing to quit; this was the beginning of the servitude of Greece to the infidels.

Therefore, let him who has no desire to conquer make use of these arms, for they are much more hazardous than mercenaries, because with them the ruin is ready made; they are all united, all yield obedience to others; but with mercenaries, when they have conquered, more time and better opportunities are needed to injure you; they are not all of one community, they are found and paid by you, and a third party, which you have made their head, is not able all at once to assume enough authority to injure you. In conclusion, in mercenaries dastardy is most dangerous; in auxiliaries, valour. The wise prince, therefore, has always avoided these arms and turned to his own; and has been willing rather to lose with them than to conquer with the others, not deeming that a real victory which is gained with the arms of others. I shall never hesitate to cite Cesare Borgia and his actions. This duke entered the Romagna with auxiliaries, taking there only French soldiers, and with them he captured Imola and Forli; but afterwards, such forces not appearing to him reliable, he turned to mercenaries, discerning less danger in them, and enlisted the Orsini and Vitelli; whom presently, on handling and finding them doubtful, unfaithful, and dangerous, he destroyed and turned to his own men. And the difference between one and the other of these forces can easily be seen when one considers the difference there was in the reputation of the duke, when he had the French, when he had the Orsini and Vitelli, and when he relied on his own soldiers, on whose fidelity he could always count and found it ever increasing; he was never esteemed more highly than when every one saw that he was complete master of his own forces.

I was not intending to go beyond Italian and recent examples, but I am unwilling to leave out Hiero, the Syracusan, he being one of those I have named above. This man, as I have said, made head of the army by the Syracusans, soon found out that a mercenary soldiery, constituted like our Italian condottieri, was of no use; and it appearing to him that he could neither keep them nor let them go, he had them all cut to pieces, and afterwards made war with his own forces and not with aliens.

I wish also to recall to memory an instance from the Old Testament applicable to this subject. David offered himself to Saul to fight with Goliath, the Philistine champion, and, to give him courage, Saul armed him with his own weapons; which David rejected as soon as he had them on his back, saying he could make no use of them, and that he wished to meet the enemy with his sling and his knife. In conclusion, the arms of others either fall from your back, or they weigh you down, or they bind you fast.

Charles the Seventh, the father of King Louis the Eleventh, having by good fortune and valour liberated France from the English, recognized the necessity of being armed with forces of his own, and he established in his kingdom ordinances concerning men-at-arms and infantry. Afterwards his son, King Louis, abolished the infantry and began to enlist the Switzers, which mistake, followed by others, is, as is now seen, a source of peril to that kingdom; because, having raised the reputation of the Switzers, he has entirely diminished the value of his own arms, for he has destroyed the infantry altogether; and his men-at-arms he has subordinated to others, for, being as they are so accustomed to fight along with Switzers, it does not appear that they can now conquer without them. Hence it arises that the French cannot stand against the Switzers, and without the Switzers they do not come off well against others. The armies of the French have thus become mixed, partly mercenary and partly national, both of which arms together are much better than mercenaries alone or auxiliaries alone, but much inferior to one's own forces. And this example proves it, for the kingdom of France would be unconquerable if the ordinance of Charles had been enlarged or maintained.

But the scanty wisdom of man, on entering into an affair which looks well at first, cannot discern the poison that is hidden in it, as I have said above of hectic fevers. Therefore, if he who rules a principality cannot recognize evils until they are upon him, he is not truly wise; and this insight is given to few. And if the first disaster to the Roman Empire should be examined, it will be found to have commenced only with the enlisting of the Goths; because from that time the vigour of the Roman Empire began to decline, and all that valour which had raised it passed away to others.

I conclude, therefore, that no principality is secure without having its own forces; on the contrary, it is entirely dependent on good fortune, not having the valour which in adversity would defend it. And it has always been the opinion and judgment of wise men that nothing can be so uncertain or unstable as fame or power not founded on its own strength. And one's own forces are those which are composed either of subjects, citizens, or dependents; all others are mercenaries or auxiliaries. And the way to make ready one's own forces will be easily found if the rules suggested by me shall be reflected upon, and if one will consider how Philip, the father of Alexander the Great, and many republics and princes have armed and organized themselves, to which rules I entirely commit myself.

CHAPTER 14

That Which Concerns a Prince on the Subject of the Art of War

A prince ought to have no other aim or thought, nor select anything else for his study, than war and its rules and discipline; for this is the sole art that belongs to him who rules, and it is of such force that it not only upholds those who are born princes, but it often enables men to rise from a private station to that rank. And, on the contrary, it is seen that when princes have thought more of ease than of arms they have lost their states. And the first cause of your losing it is to neglect this art; and what enables you to acquire a state is to be master of the art. Francesco Sforza, through being martial, from a private person became Duke of Milan; and the sons, through avoiding the hardships and troubles of arms, from dukes became private persons. For among other evils which being unarmed brings you, it causes you to be despised, and this is one of those ignominies against which a prince ought to guard himself, as is shown later on. Because there is nothing proportionate between the armed and the unarmed; and it is not reasonable that he who is armed should yield obedience willingly to him who is unarmed, or that the unarmed man should be secure among armed servants. Because, there being in the one disdain and in the other suspicion, it is not possible for them to work well together. And therefore a prince who does not understand the art of war, over and above the other misfortunes already mentioned, cannot be respected by his soldiers, nor can he rely on them. He ought never, therefore, to have out of his thoughts this subject of war, and in peace he should addict himself more to its exercise than in war; this he can do in two ways, the one by action, the other by study. As regards action, he ought above all things to keep his men well organized and drilled, to follow incessantly the chase, by which he accustoms his body to hardships, and learns something of the nature of localities, and gets to find out how the mountains rise, how the valleys open out, how the plains lie, and to understand the nature of rivers and marshes, and in all this to take the greatest care. Which knowledge is useful in two ways. Firstly, he learns to know his country, and is better able to undertake its defense; afterwards, by means of the knowledge and observation of that locality, he understands with ease any other which it may be necessary for him to study hereafter; because the hills, valleys, and plains, and rivers and marshes that are, for instance, in Tuscany, have a certain resemblance to those of other countries, so that with a knowledge of the aspect of one country one can easily arrive at a knowledge of others. And the prince that lacks this skill lacks the essential which it is desirable that a captain should possess, for it teaches him to surprise his enemy, to select quarters, to lead armies, to array the battle, to besiege towns to advantage.

Philopoemen, Prince of the Achaeans, among other praises which writers have bestowed on him, is commended because in time of peace he never had anything in his mind but the rules of war; and when he was in the country with friends, he often stopped and reasoned with them: "If the enemy should be upon that hill, and we should find ourselves here with our army, with whom would be the advantage? How should one best advance to meet him, keeping the ranks? If we should wish to retreat, how ought we to pursue?" And he would set forth to them, as he went, all the chances that could befall an army; he would listen to their opinion and state his, confirming it with reasons, so that by these continual discussions there could never arise, in time of war, any unexpected circumstances that he could not deal with.

But to exercise the intellect the prince should read histories, and study there the actions of illustrious men, to see how they have borne themselves in war, to examine the causes of their victories and defeat, so as to avoid the latter and imitate the former; and above all do as an illustrious man did, who took as an exemplar one who had been praised and famous before him, and whose achievements and deeds he always kept in his mind, as it is said Alexander the Great imitated Achilles, Caesar Alexander, Scipio Cyrus. And whoever reads the life of Cyrus, written by Xenophon, will recognize afterwards in the life of Scipio how that imitation was his glory, and how in chastity, affability, humanity, and liberality Scipio conformed to those things which have been written of Cyrus by Xenophon. A wise prince ought to observe some such rules, and never in peaceful times stand idle, but increase his resources with industry in such a way that they may be available to him in adversity, so that if fortune chances it may find him prepared to resist her blows.

CHAPTER 15

Concerning Things for Which Men, and Especially Princes, Are Praised or Blamed

It remains now to see what ought to be the rules of conduct for a prince towards subject and friends. And as I know that many have written on this point, I expect I shall be considered presumptuous in mentioning it again, especially as in discussing it I shall depart from the methods of other people. But, it being my intention to write a thing which shall be useful to him who apprehends it, it appears to me more appropriate to follow up the real truth of the matter than the imagination of it; for many have pictured republics and principalities which in fact have never been known or seen, because how one lives is so far distant from how one ought to live, that he who neglects what is done for what ought to be done, sooner effects his ruin than his preservation; for a man who wishes to act

entirely up to his professions of virtue soon
meets with what destroys him among so much
that is evil.

Hence it is necessary for a prince wishing to
hold his own to know how to do wrong, and to
make use of it or not according to necessity.
Therefore, putting on one side imaginary things
concerning a prince, and discussing those which
are real, I say that all men when they are spoken
of, and chiefly princes for being more highly
placed, are remarkable for some of those qualities
which bring them either blame or praise; and
thus it is that one is reputed liberal, another
miserly, using a Tuscan term (because an
avaricious person in our language is still he who
desires to possess by robbery, whilst we call one
miserly who deprives himself too much of the
use of his own); one is reputed generous, one
rapacious; one cruel, one compassionate; one
faithless, another faithful; one effeminate and
cowardly, another bold and brave; one affable,
another haughty; one lascivious, another chaste;
one sincere, another cunning; one hard, another
easy; one grave, another frivolous; one religious,
another unbelieving, and the like. And I know
that every one will confess that it would be most
praiseworthy in a prince to exhibit all the above
qualities that are considered good; but because

they can neither be entirely possessed nor observed, for human conditions do not permit it, it is necessary for him to be sufficiently prudent that he may know how to avoid the reproach of those vices which would lose him his state; and also to keep himself, if it be possible, from those which would not lose him it; but this not being possible, he may with less hesitation abandon himself to them. And again, he need not make himself uneasy at incurring a reproach for those vices without which the state can only be saved with difficulty, for if everything is considered carefully, it will be found that something which looks like virtue, if followed, would be his ruin; whilst something else, which looks like vice, yet followed brings him security and prosperity.

CHAPTER 16

Concerning Liberality and Meanness

Commencing then with the first of the above-named characteristics, I say that it would be well to be reputed liberal. Nevertheless, liberality exercised in a way that does not bring you the reputation for it, injures you; for if one exercises it honestly and as it should be exercised, it may not become known, and you will not avoid the reproach of its opposite. Therefore, any one wishing to maintain among men the name of liberal is obliged to avoid no attribute of magnificence; so that a prince thus inclined will consume in such acts all his property, and will be compelled in the end, if he wish to maintain the name of liberal, to unduly weigh down his people, and tax them, and do everything he can to get money. This will soon make him odious to his subjects, and becoming poor he will be little valued by any one; thus, with his liberality, having offended many and rewarded few, he is affected by the very first trouble and imperilled by whatever may be the first danger; recognizing this himself, and wishing to draw back from it, he runs at once into the reproach of being miserly.

Therefore, a prince, not being able to exercise this virtue of liberality in such a way that it is recognized, except to his cost, if he is wise he ought not to fear the reputation of being mean, for in time he will come to be more considered than if liberal, seeing that with his economy his revenues are enough, that he can defend himself against all attacks, and is able to engage in enterprises without burdening his people; thus it comes to pass that he exercises liberality towards all from whom he does not take, who are numberless, and meanness towards those to whom he does not give, who are few. We have not seen great things done in our time except by those who have been considered mean; the rest have failed. Pope Julius the Second was assisted in reaching the papacy by a reputation for liberality, yet he did not strive afterwards to keep it up, when he made war on the King of France; and he made many wars without imposing any extraordinary tax on his subjects, for he supplied his additional expenses out of his long thriftiness. The present King of Spain would not have undertaken or conquered in so many enterprises if he had been reputed liberal. A prince, therefore, provided that he has not to rob his subjects, that he can defend himself, that he does not become poor and abject, that he is not forced to become rapacious, ought to hold of little account a reputation for being mean, for it is one of those vices which will enable him to govern.

And if any one should say: Caesar obtained empire by liberality, and many others have reached the highest positions by having been liberal, and by being considered so, I answer: Either you are a prince in fact, or in a way to become one. In the first case this liberality is dangerous, in the second it is very necessary to be considered liberal; and Caesar was one of those who wished to become pre-eminent in Rome; but if he had survived after becoming so, and had not moderated his expenses, he would have destroyed his government. And if any one should reply: Many have been princes, and have done great things with armies, who have been considered very liberal, I reply: Either a prince spends that which is his own or his subjects' or else that of others. In the first case he ought to be sparing, in the second he ought not to neglect any opportunity for liberality. And to the prince who goes forth with his army, supporting it by pillage, sack, and extortion, handling that which belongs to others, this liberality is necessary, otherwise he would not be followed by soldiers. And of that which is neither yours nor your subjects' you can be a ready giver, as were Cyrus, Caesar, and Alexander; because it does not take away your reputation if you squander that of others, but adds to it; it is only squandering your own that injures you.

And there is nothing wastes so rapidly as liberality, for even whilst you exercise it you lose the power to do so, and so become either poor or despised, or else, in avoiding poverty, rapacious and hated. And a prince should guard himself, above all things, against being despised and hated; and liberality leads you to both. Therefore it is wiser to have a reputation for meanness which brings reproach without hatred, than to be compelled through seeking a reputation for liberality to incur a name for rapacity which begets reproach with hatred.

CHAPTER 17

Concerning Cruelty and Clemency, and Whether It Is Better to Be Loved Than Feared

Coming now to the other qualities mentioned above, I say that every prince ought to desire to be considered clement and not cruel.

Nevertheless he ought to take care not to misuse this clemency. Cesare Borgia was considered cruel; notwithstanding, his cruelty reconciled the Romagna, unified it, and restored it to peace and loyalty. And if this be rightly considered, he will be seen to have been much more merciful than the Florentine people, who, to avoid a reputation for cruelty, permitted Pistoia to be destroyed. Therefore a prince, so long as he keeps his subjects united and loyal, ought not to mind the reproach of cruelty; because with a few examples he will be more merciful than those who, through too much mercy, allow disorders to arise, from which follow murders or robberies;

for these are wont to injure the whole people, whilst those executions which originate with a prince offend the individual only.

And of all princes, it is impossible for the new prince to avoid the imputation of cruelty, owing to new states being full of dangers. Hence Virgil, through the mouth of Dido, excuses the inhumanity of her reign owing to its being new, saying: "Res dura, et regni novitas me talia cogunt Moliri, et late fines custode tueri." (... against my will, my fate A throne unsettled, and an infant state, Bid me defend my realms with all my powers, And guard with these severities my shores.) Nevertheless he ought to be slow to believe and to act, nor should he himself show fear, but proceed in a temperate manner with prudence and humanity, so that too much confidence may not make him incautious and too much distrust render him intolerable.

Upon this a question arises: whether it be better to be loved than feared or feared than loved? It may be answered that one should wish to be both, but, because it is difficult to unite them in one person, it is much safer to be feared than loved, when, of the two, either must be dispensed with. Because this is to be asserted in general of men, that they are ungrateful, fickle, false, cowardly, covetous, and as long as you succeed they are yours entirely; they will offer you their blood, property, life, and children, as is said above, when the need is far distant; but when it approaches they turn against you. And that prince who, relying entirely on their promises, has neglected other precautions, is ruined; because friendships that are obtained by payments, and not by greatness or nobility of mind, may indeed be earned, but they are not secured, and in time of need cannot be relied upon; and men have less scruple in offending one who is beloved than one who is feared, for love is preserved by the link of obligation which, owing to the baseness of men, is broken at every opportunity for their advantage; but fear preserves you by a dread of punishment which never fails.

Nevertheless a prince ought to inspire fear in such a way that, if he does not win love, he avoids hatred; because he can endure very well being feared whilst he is not hated, which will always be as long as he abstains from the property of his citizens and subjects and from their women. But when it is necessary for him to proceed against the life of someone, he must do it on proper justification and for manifest cause, but above all things he must keep his hands off the property of others, because men more quickly forget the death of their father than the loss of their patrimony. Besides, pretexts for taking away the property are never wanting; for he who has once begun to live by robbery will always find pretexts for seizing what belongs to others; but reasons for taking life, on the contrary, are more difficult to find and sooner lapse. But when a prince is with his army, and has under control a multitude of soldiers, then it is quite necessary for him to disregard the reputation of cruelty, for without it he would never hold his army united or disposed to its duties. Among the wonderful deeds of Hannibal this one is enumerated: that having led an enormous army, composed of many various races of men, to fight in foreign lands, no dissensions arose either among them or against the prince, whether in his bad or in his good fortune. This arose from nothing else than his inhuman cruelty, which, with his boundless valour, made him revered and terrible in the sight of his soldiers, but without that cruelty, his other virtues were not sufficient to produce this effect. And short-sighted writers admire his deeds from one point of view and from another condemn the principal cause of them. That it is true his other virtues would not have been sufficient for him may be proved by the case of Scipio, that most excellent man, not only of his own times but within the memory of man, against whom, nevertheless, his army rebelled in Spain; this arose from nothing but his too great forbearance, which gave his soldiers more license than is consistent with military discipline. For this he was upbraided in the Senate by Fabius Maximus, and called the corrupter of the Roman soldiery. The Locrians were laid waste by a legate of Scipio, yet they were not avenged by him, nor was the insolence of the legate punished, owing entirely to his easy nature. Insomuch that someone in the Senate, wishing to excuse him, said there were many men who knew much better how not to err than to correct the errors of others. This disposition, if he had been continued in the command, would have destroyed in time the fame and glory of Scipio; but, he being under the control of the Senate, this injurious characteristic not only concealed itself, but contributed to his glory.

Returning to the question of being feared or loved, I come to the conclusion that, men loving according to their own will and fearing according to that of the prince, a wise prince should establish himself on that which is in his own control and not in that of others; he must endeavor only to avoid hatred, as is noted.

CHAPTER 18

Concerning the Way in Which Princes Should Keep Faith

Every one admits how praiseworthy it is in a prince to keep faith, and to live with integrity and not with craft. Nevertheless our experience has been that those princes who have done great things have held good faith of little account, and have known how to circumvent the intellect of men by craft, and in the end have overcome those who have relied on their word. You must know there are two ways of contesting, the one by the law, the other by force; the first method is proper to men, the second to beasts; but because the first is frequently not sufficient, it is necessary to have recourse to the second. Therefore it is necessary for a prince to understand how to avail himself of the beast and the man.

This has been figuratively taught to princes by ancient writers, who describe how Achilles and many other princes of old were given to the Centaur Chiron to nurse, who brought them up

in his discipline; which means solely that, as
they had for a teacher one who was half beast
and half man, so it is necessary for a prince to
know how to make use of both natures, and that
one without the other is not durable. A prince,
therefore, being compelled knowingly to adopt
the beast, ought to choose the fox and the lion;
because the lion cannot defend himself against
snares and the fox cannot defend himself against
wolves. Therefore, it is necessary to be a fox to
discover the snares and a lion to terrify the
wolves. Those who rely simply on the lion do
not understand what they are about. Therefore a
wise lord cannot, nor ought he to, keep faith
when such observance may be turned against
him, and when the reasons that caused him to
pledge it exist no longer. If men were entirely
good this precept would not hold, but because
they are bad, and will not keep faith with you,
you too are not bound to observe it with them.
Nor will there ever be wanting to a prince
legitimate reasons to excuse this non-observance.
Of this endless modern examples could be given,
showing how many treaties and engagements
have been made void and of no effect through
the faithlessness of princes; and he who has
known best how to employ the fox has
succeeded best.

But it is necessary to know well how to disguise this characteristic, and to be a great pretender and dissembler; and men are so simple, and so subject to present necessities, that he who seeks to deceive will always find someone who will allow himself to be deceived. One recent example I cannot pass over in silence. Alexander the Sixth did nothing else but deceive men, nor ever thought of doing otherwise, and he always found victims; for there never was a man who had greater power in asserting, or who with greater oaths would affirm a thing, yet would observe it less; nevertheless his deceits always succeeded according to his wishes, because he well understood this side of mankind.

Therefore it is unnecessary for a prince to have all the good qualities I have enumerated, but it is very necessary to appear to have them. And I shall dare to say this also, that to have them and always to observe them is injurious, and that to appear to have them is useful; to appear merciful, faithful, humane, religious, upright, and to be so, but with a mind so framed that should you require not to be so, you may be able and know how to change to the opposite.

And you have to understand this, that a prince, especially a new one, cannot observe all those things for which men are esteemed, being often forced, in order to maintain the state, to act contrary to fidelity, friendship, humanity, and religion. Therefore it is necessary for him to have a mind ready to turn itself accordingly as the winds and variations of fortune force it, yet, as I have said above, not to diverge from the good if he can avoid doing so, but, if compelled, then to know how to set about it.

For this reason a prince ought to take care that he never lets anything slip from his lips that is not replete with the above-named five qualities, that he may appear to him who sees and hears him altogether merciful, faithful, humane, upright, and religious. There is nothing more necessary to appear to have than this last quality, inasmuch as men judge generally more by the eye than by the hand, because it belongs to everybody to see you, to few to come in touch with you. Every one sees what you appear to be, few really know what you are, and those few dare not oppose themselves to the opinion of the many, who have the majesty of the state to defend them; and in the actions of all men, and especially of princes, which it is not prudent to challenge, one judges by the result.

For that reason, let a prince have the credit of conquering and holding his state, the means will always be considered honest, and he will be praised by everybody; because the vulgar are always taken by what a thing seems to be and by what comes of it; and in the world there are only the vulgar, for the few find a place there only when the many have no ground to rest on.

One prince of the present time, whom it is not well to name, never preaches anything else but peace and good faith, and to both he is most hostile, and either, if he had kept it, would have deprived him of reputation and kingdom many a time.

CHAPTER 19

That One Should Avoid Being Despised and Hated

Now, concerning the characteristics of which mention is made above, I have spoken of the more important ones, the others I wish to discuss briefly under this generality, that the prince must consider, as has been in part said before, how to avoid those things which will make him hated or contemptible; and as often as he shall have succeeded he will have fulfilled his part, and he need not fear any danger in other reproaches.

It makes him hated above all things, as I have said, to be rapacious, and to be a violator of the property and women of his subjects, from both of which he must abstain. And when neither their property nor their honor is touched, the majority of men live content, and he has only to contend with the ambition of a few, whom he can curb with ease in many ways.

It makes him contemptible to be considered fickle, frivolous, effeminate, mean-spirited, irresolute, from all of which a prince should guard himself as from a rock; and he should endeavor to show in his actions greatness, courage, gravity, and fortitude; and in his private dealings with his subjects let him show that his judgments are irrevocable, and maintain himself in such reputation that no one can hope either to deceive him or to get round him.

That prince is highly esteemed who conveys this impression of himself, and he who is highly esteemed is not easily conspired against; for, provided it is well known that he is an excellent man and revered by his people, he can only be attacked with difficulty. For this reason a prince ought to have two fears, one from within, on account of his subjects, the other from without, on account of external powers. From the latter he is defended by being well armed and having good allies, and if he is well armed he will have good friends, and affairs will always remain quiet within when they are quiet without, unless they should have been already disturbed by conspiracy; and even should affairs outside be disturbed, if he has carried out his preparations and has lived as I have said, as long as he does not despair, he will resist every attack, as I said Nabis the Spartan did.

But concerning his subjects, when affairs outside are disturbed he has only to fear that they will conspire secretly, from which a prince can easily secure himself by avoiding being hated and despised, and by keeping the people satisfied with him, which it is most necessary for him to accomplish, as I said above at length. And one of the most efficacious remedies that a prince can have against conspiracies is not to be hated and despised by the people, for he who conspires against a prince always expects to please them by his removal; but when the conspirator can only look forward to offending them, he will not have the courage to take such a course, for the difficulties that confront a conspirator are infinite. And as experience shows, many have been the conspiracies, but few have been successful; because he who conspires cannot act alone, nor can he take a companion except from those whom he believes to be malcontents, and as soon as you have opened your mind to a malcontent you have given him the material with which to content himself, for by denouncing you he can look for every advantage; so that, seeing the gain from this course to be assured, and seeing the other to be doubtful and full of dangers, he must be a very rare friend, or a thoroughly obstinate enemy of the prince, to keep faith with you.

And, to reduce the matter into a small compass, I say that, on the side of the conspirator, there is nothing but fear, jealousy, prospect of punishment to terrify him; but on the side of the prince there is the majesty of the principality, the laws, the protection of friends and the state to defend him; so that, adding to all these things the popular goodwill, it is impossible that any one should be so rash as to conspire. For whereas in general the conspirator has to fear before the execution of his plot, in this case he has also to fear the sequel to the crime; because on account of it he has the people for an enemy, and thus cannot hope for any escape.

Endless examples could be given on this subject, but I will be content with one, brought to pass within the memory of our fathers. Messer Annibale Bentivogli, who was prince in Bologna (grandfather of the present Annibale), having been murdered by the Canneschi, who had conspired against him, not one of his family survived but Messer Giovanni, who was in childhood: immediately after his assassination the people rose and murdered all the Canneschi. This sprung from the popular goodwill which the house of Bentivogli enjoyed in those days in Bologna; which was so great that, although none remained there after the death of Annibale who was able to rule the state, the Bolognese, having information that there was one of the Bentivogli

family in Florence, who up to that time had been
considered the son of a blacksmith, sent to
Florence for him and gave him the government
of their city, and it was ruled by him until Messer
Giovanni came in due course to the government.

For this reason I consider that a prince ought
to reckon conspiracies of little account when his
people hold him in esteem; but when it is hostile
to him, and bears hatred towards him, he ought to
fear everything and everybody. And well-ordered
states and wise princes have taken every care not
to drive the nobles to desperation, and to keep the
people satisfied and contented, for this is one of
the most important objects a prince can have.

Among the best ordered and governed
kingdoms of our times is France, and in it are
found many good institutions on which depend
the liberty and security of the king; of these the
first is the parliament and its authority, because
he who founded the kingdom, knowing the
ambition of the nobility and their boldness,
considered that a bit to their mouths would be
necessary to hold them in; and, on the other side,
knowing the hatred of the people, founded in
fear, against the nobles, he wished to protect
them, yet he was not anxious for this to be the
particular care of the king; therefore, to take
away the reproach which he would be liable to

from the nobles for favoring the people, and from the people for favoring the nobles, he set up an arbiter, who should be one who could beat down the great and favor the lesser without reproach to the king. Neither could you have a better or a more prudent arrangement, or a greater source of security to the king and kingdom. From this one can draw another important conclusion, that princes ought to leave affairs of reproach to the management of others, and keep those of grace in their own hands. And further, I consider that a prince ought to cherish the nobles, but not so as to make himself hated by the people.

It may appear, perhaps, to some who have examined the lives and deaths of the Roman emperors that many of them would be an example contrary to my opinion, seeing that some of them lived nobly and showed great qualities of soul, nevertheless they have lost their empire or have been killed by subjects who have conspired against them. Wishing, therefore, to answer these objections, I will recall the characters of some of the emperors, and will show that the causes of their ruin were not different to those alleged by me; at the same time I will only submit for consideration those things that are noteworthy to him who studies the affairs of those times.

It seems to me sufficient to take all those emperors who succeeded to the empire from Marcus the philosopher down to Maximinus; they were Marcus and his son Commodus, Pertinax, Julian, Severus and his son Antoninus Caracalla, Macrinus, Heliogabalus, Alexander, and Maximinus. There is first to note that, whereas in other principalities the ambition of the nobles and the insolence of the people only have to be contended with, the Roman emperors had a third difficulty in having to put up with the cruelty and avarice of their soldiers, a matter so beset with difficulties that it was the ruin of many; for it was a hard thing to give satisfaction both to soldiers and people; because the people loved peace, and for this reason they loved the unaspiring prince, whilst the soldiers loved the warlike prince who was bold, cruel, and rapacious, which qualities they were quite willing he should exercise upon the people, so that they could get double pay and give vent to their own greed and cruelty. Hence it arose that those emperors were always overthrown who, either by birth or training, had no great authority, and most of them, especially those who came new to the principality, recognizing the difficulty of these two opposing humors, were inclined to give satisfaction to the soldiers, caring little about injuring the people. Which course was necessary, because, as princes cannot help being hated by someone, they ought, in the first place, to avoid being hated by every one, and when they cannot compass this, they ought to endeavor with the utmost diligence to avoid the hatred of the most powerful. Therefore, those emperors who through inexperience had need of special favor adhered more readily to the soldiers than to the people; a course which turned out advantageous to them or not, accordingly as the prince knew how to maintain authority over them.

From these causes it arose that Marcus, Pertinax, and Alexander, being all men of modest life, lovers of justice, enemies to cruelty, humane, and benignant, came to a sad end except Marcus; he alone lived and died honored, because he had succeeded to the throne by hereditary title, and owed nothing either to the soldiers or the people; and afterwards, being possessed of many virtues which made him respected, he always kept both orders in their places whilst he lived, and was neither hated nor despised.

But Pertinax was created emperor against the wishes of the soldiers, who, being accustomed to live licentiously under Commodus, could not endure the honest life to which Pertinax wished to reduce them; thus, having given cause for hatred, to which hatred there was added contempt for his old age, he was overthrown at the very beginning of his administration. And here it should be noted that hatred is acquired as much by good works as by bad ones, therefore, as I said before, a prince wishing to keep his state is very often forced to do evil; for when that body is corrupt whom you think you have need of to maintain yourself—it may be either the people or the soldiers or the nobles—you have to submit to its humors and to gratify them, and then good works will do you harm.

But let us come to Alexander, who was a man of such great goodness, that among the other praises which are accorded him is this, that in the fourteen years he held the empire no one was ever put to death by him unjudged; nevertheless, being considered effeminate and a man who allowed himself to be governed by his mother, he became despised, the army conspired against him, and murdered him. Turning now to the opposite characters of Commodus, Severus, Antoninus Caracalla, and Maximinus, you will find them all cruel and rapacious—men who, to satisfy their soldiers, did not hesitate to commit every kind of iniquity against the people; and all, except Severus, came to a bad end; but in Severus there was so much valour that, keeping the soldiers friendly, although the people were oppressed by him, he reigned successfully; for his valour made him so much admired in the sight of the soldiers and people that the latter were kept in a way astonished and awed and the former respectful and satisfied. And because the actions of this man, as a new prince, were great, I wish to show briefly that he knew well how to counterfeit the fox and the lion, which natures, as I said above, it is necessary for a prince to imitate.

Knowing the sloth of the Emperor Julian, he persuaded the army in Sclavonia, of which he was captain, that it would be right to go to Rome and avenge the death of Pertinax, who had been killed by the praetorian soldiers; and under this pretext, without appearing to aspire to the throne, he moved the army on Rome, and reached Italy before it was known that he had started. On his arrival at Rome, the Senate, through fear, elected him emperor and killed Julian. After this there remained for Severus, who wished to make himself master of the whole empire, two difficulties; one in Asia, where Niger, head of the Asiatic army, had caused himself to be proclaimed emperor; the other in the west where Albinus was, who also aspired to the throne. And as he considered it dangerous to declare himself hostile to both, he decided to attack Niger and to deceive Albinus. To the latter he wrote that, being elected emperor by the Senate, he was willing to share that dignity with him and sent him the title of Caesar; and, moreover, that the Senate had made Albinus his colleague; which things were accepted by Albinus as true. But after Severus had conquered and killed Niger, and settled oriental affairs, he returned to Rome and complained to the Senate that Albinus, little recognizing the benefits that he had received from him, had by treachery sought to murder him, and for this ingratitude he was compelled to punish him. Afterwards he sought him out in France, and took from him his government and life. He who will, therefore, carefully examine the actions of this man will find him a most valiant lion and a most cunning fox; he will find him feared and respected by every one, and not hated by the army; and it need not be wondered at that he, a new man, was able to hold the empire so well, because his supreme renown always protected him from that hatred which the people might have conceived against him for his violence.

But his son Antoninus was a most eminent man, and had very excellent qualities, which made him admirable in the sight of the people and acceptable to the soldiers, for he was a warlike man, most enduring of fatigue, a despiser of all delicate food and other luxuries, which caused him to be beloved by the armies. Nevertheless, his ferocity and cruelties were so great and so unheard of that, after endless single murders, he killed a large number of the people of Rome and all those of Alexandria. He became hated by the whole world, and also feared by those he had around him, to such an extent that he was murdered in the midst of his army by a centurion. And here it must be noted that such like deaths, which are deliberately inflicted with a resolved and desperate courage, cannot be avoided by princes, because any one who does not fear to die can inflict them; but a prince may fear them the less because they are very rare; he has only to be careful not to do any grave injury to those whom he employs or has around him in the service of the state. Antoninus had not taken this care, but had contumeliously killed a brother of that centurion, whom also he daily threatened, yet retained in his bodyguard; which, as it turned out, was a rash thing to do, and proved the emperor's ruin.

But let us come to Commodus, to whom it should have been very easy to hold the empire, for, being the son of Marcus, he had inherited it, and he had only to follow in the footsteps of his father to please his people and soldiers; but, being by nature cruel and brutal, he gave himself up to amusing the soldiers and corrupting them, so that he might indulge his rapacity upon the people; on the other hand, not maintaining his dignity, often descending to the theatre to compete with gladiators, and doing other vile things, little worthy of the imperial majesty, he fell into contempt with the soldiers, and being hated by one party and despised by the other, he was conspired against and was killed.

It remains to discuss the character of Maximinus. He was a very warlike man, and the armies, being disgusted with the effeminacy of Alexander, of whom I have already spoken, killed him and elected Maximinus to the throne. This he did not possess for long, for two things made him hated and despised; the one, his having kept sheep in Thrace, which brought him into contempt (it being well known to all, and considered a great indignity by every one), and the other, his having at the accession to his dominions deferred going to Rome and taking possession of the imperial seat; he had also gained a reputation for the utmost ferocity by having, through his prefects in Rome and elsewhere in the empire, practiced many cruelties, so that the whole world was moved to

anger at the meanness of his birth and to fear at
his barbarity. First Africa rebelled, then the
Senate with all the people of Rome, and all Italy
conspired against him, to which may be added
his own army; this latter, besieging Aquileia and
meeting with difficulties in taking it, were
disgusted with his cruelties, and fearing him less
when they found so many against him, murdered
him. I do not wish to discuss Heliogabalus,
Macrinus, or Julian, who, being thoroughly
contemptible, were quickly wiped out; but I will
bring this discourse to a conclusion by saying
that princes in our times have this difficulty of
giving inordinate satisfaction to their soldiers in a
far less degree, because, notwithstanding one has
to give them some indulgence, that is soon done;
none of these princes have armies that are
veterans in the governance and administration of
provinces, as were the armies of the Roman
Empire; and whereas it was then more necessary
to give satisfaction to the soldiers than to the
people, it is now more necessary to all princes,
except the Turk and the Soldan, to satisfy the
people rather the soldiers, because the people are
the more powerful.

From the above I have excepted the Turk, who
always keeps round him twelve thousand
infantry and fifteen thousand cavalry on which

depend the security and strength of the kingdom,
and it is necessary that, putting aside every
consideration for the people, he should keep
them his friends. The kingdom of the Soldan is
similar; being entirely in the hands of soldiers, it
follows again that, without regard to the people,
he must keep them his friends. But you must
note that the state of the Soldan is unlike all other
principalities, for the reason that it is like the
Christian pontificate, which cannot be called
either an hereditary or a newly formed
principality; because the sons of the old prince
are not the heirs, but he who is elected to that
position by those who have authority, and the
sons remain only noblemen. And this being an
ancient custom, it cannot be called a new
principality, because there are none of those
difficulties in it that are met with in new ones; for
although the prince is new, the constitution of the
state is old, and it is framed so as to receive him
as if he were its hereditary lord.

But returning to the subject of our discourse, I
say that whoever will consider it will
acknowledge that either hatred or contempt has
been fatal to the above-named emperors, and it
will be recognized also how it happened that, a
number of them acting in one way and a number
in another, only one in each way came to a

happy end and the rest to unhappy ones.
Because it would have been useless and
dangerous for Pertinax and Alexander, being
new princes, to imitate Marcus, who was heir to
the principality; and likewise it would have been
utterly destructive to Caracalla, Commodus, and
Maximinus to have imitated Severus, they not
having sufficient valour to enable them to tread
in his footsteps. Therefore a prince, new to the
principality, cannot imitate the actions of
Marcus, nor, again, is it necessary to follow those
of Severus, but he ought to take from Severus
those parts which are necessary to found his
state, and from Marcus those which are proper
and glorious to keep a state that may already be
stable and firm.

CHAPTER 20

Are Fortresses, and Many Other Things to Which Princes Often Resort, Advantageous or Hurtful?

1. Some princes, so as to hold securely the state, have disarmed their subjects; others have kept their subject towns distracted by factions; others have fostered enmities against themselves; others have laid themselves out to gain over those whom they distrusted in the beginning of their governments; some have built fortresses; some have overthrown and destroyed them. And although one cannot give a final judgment on all of these things unless one possesses the particulars of those states in which a decision has to be made, nevertheless I will speak as comprehensively as the matter of itself will admit.

2. There never was a new prince who has disarmed his subjects; rather when he has found

them disarmed he has always armed them,
because, by arming them, those arms become
yours, those men who were distrusted become
faithful, and those who were faithful are kept so,
and your subjects become your adherents. And
whereas all subjects cannot be armed, yet when
those whom you do arm are benefited, the others
can be handled more freely, and this difference in
their treatment, which they quite understand,
makes the former your dependents, and the
latter, considering it to be necessary that those
who have the most danger and service should
have the most reward, excuse you. But when you
disarm them, you at once offend them by
showing that you distrust them, either for
cowardice or for want of loyalty, and either of
these opinions breeds hatred against you. And
because you cannot remain unarmed, it follows
that you turn to mercenaries, which are of the
character already shown; even if they should be
good they would not be sufficient to defend you
against powerful enemies and distrusted subjects.
Therefore, as I have said, a new prince in a new
principality has always distributed arms.
Histories are full of examples. But when a prince
acquires a new state, which he adds as a province
to his old one, then it is necessary to disarm the
men of that state, except those who have been his

adherents in acquiring it; and these again, with time and opportunity, should be rendered soft and effeminate; and matters should be managed in such a way that all the armed men in the state shall be your own soldiers who in your old state were living near you.

3. Our forefathers, and those who were reckoned wise, were accustomed to say that it was necessary to hold Pistoia by factions and Pisa by fortresses; and with this idea they fostered quarrels in some of their tributary towns so as to keep possession of them the more easily. This may have been well enough in those times when Italy was in a way balanced, but I do not believe that it can be accepted as a precept for today, because I do not believe that factions can ever be of use; rather it is certain that when the enemy comes upon you in divided cities you are quickly lost, because the weakest party will always assist the outside forces and the other will not be able to resist. The Venetians, moved, as I believe, by the above reasons, fostered the Guelph and Ghibelline factions in their tributary cities; and although they never allowed them to come to bloodshed, yet they nursed these disputes amongst them, so that the citizens, distracted by their differences, should not unite

against them. Which, as we saw, did not afterwards turn out as expected, because, after the rout at Vaila, one party at once took courage and seized the state. Such methods argue, therefore, weakness in the prince, because these factions will never be permitted in a vigorous principality; such methods for enabling one the more easily to manage subjects are only useful in times of peace, but if war comes this policy proves fallacious.

4. Without doubt princes become great when they overcome the difficulties and obstacles by which they are confronted, and therefore fortune, especially when she desires to make a new prince great, who has a greater necessity to earn renown than an hereditary one, causes enemies to arise and form designs against him, in order that he may have the opportunity of overcoming them, and by them to mount higher, as by a ladder which his enemies have raised. For this reason many consider that a wise prince, when he has the opportunity, ought with craft to foster some animosity against himself, so that, having crushed it, his renown may rise higher.

5. Princes, especially new ones, have found more fidelity and assistance in those men who in

the beginning of their rule were distrusted than among those who in the beginning were trusted. Pandolfo Petrucci, Prince of Siena, ruled his state more by those who had been distrusted than by others. But on this question one cannot speak generally, for it varies so much with the individual; I will only say this, that those men who at the commencement of a princedom have been hostile, if they are of a description to need assistance to support themselves, can always be gained over with the greatest ease, and they will be tightly held to serve the prince with fidelity, inasmuch as they know it to be very necessary for them to cancel by deeds the bad impression which he had formed of them; and thus the prince always extracts more profit from them than from those who, serving him in too much security, may neglect his affairs. And since the matter demands it, I must not fail to warn a prince, who by means of secret favors has acquired a new state, that he must well consider the reasons which induced those to favor him who did so; and if it be not a natural affection towards him, but only discontent with their government, then he will only keep them friendly with great trouble and difficulty, for it will be impossible to satisfy them. And weighing well the reasons for this in those examples which can be taken from ancient and modern affairs, we shall find that it is easier for the prince to make friends of those men who were contented under the former government, and are therefore his enemies, than of those who, being discontented with it, were favorable to him and encouraged him to seize it.

6. It has been a custom with princes, in order to hold their states more securely, to build fortresses that may serve as a bridle and bit to those who might design to work against them, and as a place of refuge from a first attack. I praise this system because it has been made use of formerly. Notwithstanding that, Messer Nicolo Vitelli in our times has been seen to demolish two fortresses in Citta di Castello so that he might keep that state; Guido Ubaldo, Duke of Urbino, on returning to his dominion, whence he had been driven by Cesare Borgia, razed to the foundations all the fortresses in that province, and considered that without them it would be more difficult to lose it; the Bentivogli returning to Bologna came to a similar decision. Fortresses, therefore, are useful or not according to circumstances; if they do you good in one way they injure you in another. And this question can be reasoned thus: the prince who has more to

fear from the people than from foreigners ought to build fortresses, but he who has more to fear from foreigners than from the people ought to leave them alone. The castle of Milan, built by Francesco Sforza, has made, and will make, more trouble for the house of Sforza than any other disorder in the state. For this reason the best possible fortress is not to be hated by the people, because, although you may hold the fortresses, yet they will not save you if the people hate you, for there will never be wanting foreigners to assist a people who have taken arms against you. It has not been seen in our times that such fortresses have been of use to any prince, unless to the Countess of Forli, when the Count Girolamo, her consort, was killed; for by that means she was able to withstand the popular attack and wait for assistance from Milan, and thus recover her state; and the posture of affairs was such at that time that the foreigners could not assist the people. But fortresses were of little value to her afterwards when Cesare Borgia attacked her, and when the people, her enemy, were allied with foreigners. Therefore, it would have been safer for her, both then and before, not to have been hated by the people than to have had the fortresses. All these things considered then, I shall praise him who builds fortresses as well as him who does not, and I shall blame whoever, trusting in them, cares little about being hated by the people.

CHAPTER 21

How a Prince Should Conduct Himself So As To Gain Renown

Nothing makes a prince so much esteemed as great enterprises and setting a fine example. We have in our time Ferdinand of Aragon, the present King of Spain. He can almost be called a new prince, because he has risen, by fame and glory, from being an insignificant king to be the foremost king in Christendom; and if you will consider his deeds you will find them all great and some of them extraordinary. In the beginning of his reign he attacked Granada, and this enterprise was the foundation of his dominions. He did this quietly at first and without any fear of hindrance, for he held the minds of the barons of Castile occupied in thinking of the war and not anticipating any innovations; thus they did not perceive that by these means he was acquiring power and authority over them. He was able with the money of the Church and of the people to sustain his armies, and by that long

war to lay the foundation for the military skill
which has since distinguished him. Further,
always using religion as a plea, so as to
undertake greater schemes, he devoted himself
with pious cruelty to driving out and clearing his
kingdom of the Moors; nor could there be a more
admirable example, nor one more rare. Under
this same cloak he assailed Africa, he came down
on Italy, he has finally attacked France; and thus
his achievements and designs have always been
great, and have kept the minds of his people in
suspense and admiration and occupied with the
issue of them. And his actions have arisen in such
a way, one out of the other, that men have never
been given time to work steadily against him.

Again, it much assists a prince to set unusual
examples in internal affairs, similar to those
which are related of Messer Bernabo da Milano,
who, when he had the opportunity, by any one in
civil life doing some extraordinary thing, either
good or bad, would take some method of
rewarding or punishing him, which would be
much spoken about. And a prince ought, above
all things, always endeavor in every action to
gain for himself the reputation of being a great
and remarkable man.

A prince is also respected when he is either a
true friend or a downright enemy, that is to say,

when, without any reservation, he declares himself in favor of one party against the other; which course will always be more advantageous than standing neutral; because if two of your powerful neighbors come to blows, they are of such a character that, if one of them conquers, you have either to fear him or not. In either case it will always be more advantageous for you to declare yourself and to make war strenuously; because, in the first case, if you do not declare yourself, you will invariably fall a prey to the conqueror, to the pleasure and satisfaction of him who has been conquered, and you will have no reasons to offer, nor anything to protect or to shelter you. Because he who conquers does not want doubtful friends who will not aid him in the time of trial; and he who loses will not harbor you because you did not willingly, sword in hand, court his fate.

Antiochus went into Greece, being sent for by the Aetolians to drive out the Romans. He sent envoys to the Achaeans, who were friends of the Romans, exhorting them to remain neutral; and on the other hand the Romans urged them to take up arms. This question came to be discussed in the council of the Achaeans, where the legate of Antiochus urged them to stand neutral. To this the Roman legate answered: "As for that which has been said, that it is better and more advantageous for your state not to interfere in our war, nothing can be more erroneous; because by not interfering you will be left, without favor or consideration, the guerdon of the conqueror." Thus it will always happen that he who is not your friend will demand your neutrality, whilst he who is your friend will entreat you to declare yourself with arms. And irresolute princes, to avoid present dangers, generally follow the neutral path, and are generally ruined. But when a prince declares himself gallantly in favor of one side, if the party with whom he allies himself conquers, although the victor may be powerful and may have him at his mercy, yet he is indebted to him, and there is established a bond of amity; and men are never so shameless as to become a monument of ingratitude by oppressing you. Victories after all are never so complete that the victor must not show some regard, especially to justice. But if he with whom you ally yourself loses, you may be sheltered by him, and whilst he is able he may aid you, and you become companions on a fortune that may rise again. In the second case, when those who fight are of such a character that you have no anxiety as to who may conquer, so much the more is it greater prudence to be allied, because you assist at the destruction of one by the aid of another who, if he had been wise, would have saved him; and conquering, as it is impossible that he should not do with your assistance, he remains at your discretion. And here it is to be noted that a prince ought to take care never to make an alliance with one more powerful than himself for the purposes of attacking others, unless necessity compels him, as is said above; because if he conquers you are at his discretion, and princes ought to avoid as much as possible being at the discretion of any one. The Venetians joined with France against the Duke of Milan, and this alliance, which caused their ruin, could have been avoided. But when it cannot be avoided, as happened to the Florentines when the Pope and Spain sent armies to attack Lombardy, then in such a case, for the above reasons, the prince ought to favor one of the parties.

Never let any Government imagine that it can choose perfectly safe courses; rather let it expect to have to take very doubtful ones, because it is found in ordinary affairs that one never seeks to avoid one trouble without running into another; but prudence consists in knowing how to distinguish the character of troubles, and for choice to take the lesser evil.

A prince ought also to show himself a patron of ability, and to honor the proficient in every art. At the same time he should encourage his citizens to practice their callings peaceably, both in commerce and agriculture, and in every other following, so that the one should not be deterred from improving his possessions for fear lest they be taken away from him or another from opening up trade for fear of taxes; but the prince ought to offer rewards to whoever wishes to do these things and designs in any way to honor his city or state.

Further, he ought to entertain the people with festivals and spectacles at convenient seasons of the year; and as every city is divided into guilds or into societies, he ought to hold such bodies in esteem, and associate with them sometimes, and show himself an example of courtesy and liberality; nevertheless, always maintaining the majesty of his rank, for this he must never consent to abate in anything.

CHAPTER 22

Concerning the Secretaries of Princes

The choice of servants is of no little importance to a prince, and they are good or not according to the discrimination of the prince. And the first opinion which one forms of a prince, and of his understanding, is by observing the men he has around him; and when they are capable and faithful he may always be considered wise, because he has known how to recognize the capable and to keep them faithful. But when they are otherwise one cannot form a good opinion of him, for the prime error which he made was in choosing them. There were none who knew Messer Antonio da Venafro as the servant of Pandolfo Petrucci, Prince of Siena, who would not consider Pandolfo to be a very clever man in having Venafro for his servant. Because there are three classes of intellects: one which comprehends by itself; another which appreciates what others comprehended; and a third which neither comprehends by itself nor by the showing of others; the first is the most excellent, the second is good, the third is useless. Therefore, it follows necessarily that, if Pandolfo was not in the first rank, he was in the second, for whenever one has judgment to know good and bad when it is said and done, although he himself may not have the initiative, yet he can recognize the good and the bad in his servant, and the one he can praise and the other correct; thus the servant cannot hope to deceive him, and is kept honest.

But to enable a prince to form an opinion of his servant there is one test which never fails; when you see the servant thinking more of his own interests than of yours, and seeking inwardly his own profit in everything, such a man will never make a good servant, nor will you ever be able to trust him; because he who has the state of another in his hands ought never to think of himself, but always of his prince, and never pay any attention to matters in which the prince is not concerned.

On the other hand, to keep his servant honest the prince ought to study him, honoring him, enriching him, doing him kindnesses, sharing with him the honors and cares; and at the same time let him see that he cannot stand alone, so that many honors may not make him desire

more, many riches make him wish for more, and
that many cares may make him dread chances.
When, therefore, servants, and princes towards
servants, are thus disposed, they can trust each
other, but when it is otherwise, the end will
always be disastrous for either one or the other.

CHAPTER 23

How Flatterers Should be Avoided

I do not wish to leave out an important branch of this subject, for it is a danger from which princes are with difficulty preserved, unless they are very careful and discriminating. It is that of flatterers, of whom courts are full, because men are so self-complacent in their own affairs, and in a way so deceived in them, that they are preserved with difficulty from this pest, and if they wish to defend themselves they run the danger of falling into contempt. Because there is no other way of guarding oneself from flatterers except letting men understand that to tell you the truth does not offend you; but when every one may tell you the truth, respect for you abates.

Therefore a wise prince ought to hold a third course by choosing the wise men in his state, and giving to them only the liberty of speaking the truth to him, and then only of those things of which he inquires, and of none others; but he ought to question them upon everything, and

listen to their opinions, and afterwards form his
own conclusions. With these councillors,
separately and collectively, he ought to carry
himself in such a way that each of them should
know that, the more freely he shall speak, the
more he shall be preferred; outside of these, he
should listen to no one, pursue the thing resolved
on, and be steadfast in his resolutions. He who
does otherwise is either overthrown by flatterers,
or is so often changed by varying opinions that
he falls into contempt.

I wish on this subject to adduce a modern
example. Fra Luca, the man of affairs to
Maximilian, the present emperor, speaking of his
majesty, said: He consulted with no one, yet
never got his own way in anything. This arose
because of his following a practice the opposite
to the above; for the emperor is a secretive man—
he does not communicate his designs to any one,
nor does he receive opinions on them. But as in
carrying them into effect they become revealed
and known, they are at once obstructed by those
men whom he has around him, and he, being
pliant, is diverted from them. Hence it follows
that those things he does one day he undoes the
next, and no one ever understands what he
wishes or intends to do, and no one can rely on
his resolutions.

A prince, therefore, ought always to take counsel, but only when he wishes and not when others wish; he ought rather to discourage every one from offering advice unless he asks it; but, however, he ought to be a constant inquirer, and afterwards a patient listener concerning the things of which he inquired; also, on learning that nay one, on any consideration, has not told him the truth, he should let his anger be felt.

And if there are some who think that a prince who conveys an impression of his wisdom is not so through his own ability, but through the good advisers that he has around him, beyond doubt they are deceived, because this is an axiom which never fails: that a prince who is not wise himself will never take good advice, unless by chance he has yielded his affairs entirely to one person who happens to be a very prudent man. In this case indeed he may be well governed, but it would not be for long, because such a governor would in a short time take away his state from him.

But if a prince who is not inexperienced should take counsel from more than one he will never get united counsels, nor will he know how to unite them. Each of the counselors will think of his own interests, and the prince will not know how to control them or to see through them. And they are not to found otherwise, because men will always prove untrue to you unless they are kept honest by constraint. Therefore it must be inferred that good counsels, whencesoever they come, are born of the wisdom of the prince, and not the wisdom of the prince from good counsels.

CHAPTER 24

Why the Princes of Italy Have Lost Their States

The previous suggestions, carefully observed, will enable a new prince to appear well established, and render him at once more secure and fixed in the state than if he had been long seated there. For the actions of a new prince are more narrowly observed than those of an hereditary one, and when they are seen to be able they gain more men and bind far tighter than ancient blood; because men are attracted more by the present than by the past, and when they find the present good they enjoy it and seek no further; they will also make the utmost defense of a prince if he fails them not in other things. Thus it will be a double glory for him to have established a new principality, and adorned and strengthened it with good laws, good arms, good allies, and with a good example; so will it be a double disgrace to him who, born a prince, shall lose his state by want of wisdom.

And if those seigniors are considered who have lost their states in Italy in our times, such as the King of Naples, the Duke of Milan, and others, there will be found in them, firstly, one common defect in regard to arms from the causes which have been discussed at length; in the next place, some one of them will be seen, either to have had the people hostile, or if he has had the people friendly, he has not known how to secure the nobles. In the absence of these defects states that have power enough to keep an army in the field cannot be lost.

Philip of Macedon, not the father of Alexander the Great, but he who was conquered by Titus Quintius, had not much territory compared to the greatness of the Romans and of Greece who attacked him, yet being a warlike man who knew how to attract the people and secure the nobles, he sustained the war against his enemies for many years, and if in the end he lost the dominion of some cities, nevertheless he retained the kingdom.

Therefore, do not let our princes accuse fortune for the loss of their principalities after so many years' possession, but rather their own sloth, because in quiet times they never thought there could be a change (it is a common defect in man not to make any provision in the calm against the tempest), and when afterwards the bad times came they thought of flight and not of defending themselves, and they hoped that the people, disgusted with the insolence of the conquerors, would recall them. This course, when others fail, may be good, but it is very bad to have neglected all other expedients for that, since you would never wish to fall because you trusted to be able to find someone later on to restore you. This again either does not happen, or, if it does, it will not be for your security, because that deliverance is of no avail which does not depend upon yourself; those only are reliable, certain, and durable that depend on yourself and your valour.

CHAPTER 25

What Fortune Can Effect in Human Affairs and How to Withstand Her

It is not unknown to me how many men have had, and still have, the opinion that the affairs of the world are in such wise governed by fortune and by God that men with their wisdom cannot direct them and that no one can even help them; and because of this they would have us believe that it is not necessary to labor much in affairs, but to let chance govern them. This opinion has been more credited in our times because of the great changes in affairs which have been seen, and may still be seen, every day, beyond all human conjecture.

Sometimes pondering over this, I am in some degree inclined to their opinion. Nevertheless, not to extinguish our free will, I hold it to be true that Fortune is the arbiter of one-half of our actions, but that she still leaves us to direct the other half, or perhaps a little less.

I compare her to one of those raging rivers,

which when in flood overflows the plains, sweeping away trees and buildings, bearing away the soil from place to place; everything flies before it, all yield to its violence, without being able in any way to withstand it; and yet, though its nature be such, it does not follow therefore that men, when the weather becomes fair, shall not make provision, both with defenses and barriers, in such a manner that, rising again, the waters may pass away by canal, and their force be neither so unrestrained nor so dangerous. So it happens with fortune, who shows her power where valour has not prepared to resist her, and thither she turns her forces where she knows that barriers and defenses have not been raised to constrain her.

And if you will consider Italy, which is the seat of these changes, and which has given to them their impulse, you will see it to be an open country without barriers and without any defense. For if it had been defended by proper valour, as are Germany, Spain, and France, either this invasion would not have made the great changes it has made or it would not have come at all. And this I consider enough to say concerning resistance to fortune in general.

But confining myself more to the particular, I say that a prince may be seen happy today and ruined tomorrow without having shown any change of disposition or character. This, I believe, arises firstly from causes that have already been discussed at length, namely, that the prince who relies entirely on fortune is lost when it changes. I believe also that he will be successful who directs his actions according to the spirit of the times, and that he whose actions do not accord with the times will not be successful. Because men are seen, in affairs that lead to the end which every man has before him, namely, glory and riches, to get there by various methods; one with caution, another with haste; one by force, another by skill; one by patience, another by its opposite; and each one succeeds in reaching the goal by a different method. One can also see of two cautious men the one attain his end, the other fail; and similarly, two men by different observances are equally successful, the one being cautious, the other impetuous; all this arises from nothing else than whether or not they conform in their methods to the spirit of the times. This follows from what I have said, that two men working differently bring about the same effect, and of two working similarly, one attains his object and the other does not.

Changes in estate also issue from this, for if, to one who governs himself with caution and patience, times and affairs converge in such a way that his administration is successful, his fortune is made; but if times and affairs change, he is ruined if he does not change his course of action. But a man is not often found sufficiently circumspect to know how to accommodate himself to the change, both because he cannot deviate from what nature inclines him to do, and also because, having always prospered by acting in one way, he cannot be persuaded that it is well to leave it; and, therefore, the cautious man, when it is time to turn adventurous, does not know how to do it, hence he is ruined; but had he changed his conduct with the times, fortune would not have changed.

Pope Julius the Second went to work impetuously in all his affairs, and found the times and circumstances conform so well to that line of action that he always met with success. Consider his first enterprise against Bologna, Messer Giovanni Bentivogli being still alive. The Venetians were not agreeable to it, nor was the King of Spain, and he had the enterprise still under discussion with the King of France; nevertheless he personally entered upon the expedition with his accustomed boldness and energy, a move which made Spain and the Venetians stand irresolute and passive, the latter from fear, the former from desire to recover the kingdom of Naples; on the other hand, he drew after him the King of France, because that king, having observed the movement, and desiring to make the Pope his friend so as to humble the Venetians, found it impossible to refuse him. Therefore Julius with his impetuous action accomplished what no other pontiff with simple human wisdom could have done; for if he had waited in Rome until he could get away, with his plans arranged and everything fixed, as any other pontiff would have done, he would never have succeeded. Because the King of France would have made a thousand excuses, and the others would have raised a thousand fears.

I will leave his other actions alone, as they were all alike, and they all succeeded, for the shortness of his life did not let him experience the contrary; but if circumstances had arisen which required him to go cautiously, his ruin would have followed, because he would never have deviated from those ways to which nature inclined him.

I conclude, therefore that, fortune being changeful and mankind steadfast in their ways, so long as the two are in agreement men are successful, but unsuccessful when they fall out. For my part I consider that it is better to be adventurous than cautious, because fortune is a woman, and if you wish to keep her under it is necessary to beat and ill-use her; and it is seen that she allows herself to be mastered by the adventurous rather than by those who go to work more coldly. She is, therefore, always, woman-like, a lover of young men, because they are less cautious, more violent, and with more audacity command her.

CHAPTER 26

An Exhortation to Liberate Italy From the Barbarians

Having carefully considered the subject of the above discourses, and wondering within myself whether the present times were propitious to a new prince, and whether there were elements that would give an opportunity to a wise and virtuous one to introduce a new order of things which would do honor to him and good to the people of this country, it appears to me that so many things concur to favor a new prince that I never knew a time more fit than the present.

And if, as I said, it was necessary that the people of Israel should be captive so as to make manifest the ability of Moses; that the Persians should be oppressed by the Medes so as to discover the greatness of the soul of Cyrus; and that the Athenians should be dispersed to illustrate the capabilities of Theseus: then at the present time, in order to discover the virtue of an Italian spirit, it was necessary that Italy should be reduced to the extremity that she is now in, that she should be more enslaved than the Hebrews, more oppressed than the Persians, more scattered than the Athenians; without head, without order, beaten, despoiled, torn, overrun; and to have endured every kind of desolation.

Although lately some spark may have been shown by one, which made us think he was ordained by God for our redemption, nevertheless it was afterwards seen, in the height of his career, that fortune rejected him; so that Italy, left as without life, waits for him who shall yet heal her wounds and put an end to the ravaging and plundering of Lombardy, to the swindling and taxing of the kingdom and of Tuscany, and cleanse those sores that for long have festered. It is seen how she entreats God to send someone who shall deliver her from these wrongs and barbarous insolencies. It is seen also that she is ready and willing to follow a banner if only someone will raise it.

Nor is there to be seen at present one in whom she can place more hope than in your illustrious house, with its valour and fortune, favored by God and by the Church of which it is now the chief, and which could be made the head of this redemption. This will not be difficult if you will recall to yourself the actions and lives of the men I have named. And although they were great and wonderful men, yet they were men, and each one of them had no more opportunity than the present offers, for their enterprises were neither more just nor easier than this, nor was God more their friend than He is yours.

With us there is great justice, because that war is just which is necessary, and arms are hallowed when there is no other hope but in them. Here there is the greatest willingness, and where the willingness is great the difficulties cannot be great if you will only follow those men to whom I have directed your attention. Further than this, how extraordinarily the ways of God have been manifested beyond example: the sea is divided, a cloud has led the way, the rock has poured forth water, it has rained manna, everything has contributed to your greatness; you ought to do the rest. God is not willing to do everything, and thus take away our free will and that share of glory which belongs to us.

And it is not to be wondered at if none of the above-named Italians have been able to accomplish all that is expected from your illustrious house; and if in so many revolutions in Italy, and in so many campaigns, it has always appeared as if military virtue were exhausted, this has happened because the old order of things was not good, and none of us have known how to find a new one. And nothing honors a man more than to establish new laws and new ordinances when he himself was newly risen. Such things when they are well founded and dignified will make him revered and admired, and in Italy there are not wanting opportunities to bring such into use in every form. Here there is great valour in the limbs whilst it fails in the head. Look attentively at the duels and the hand-to-hand combats, how superior the Italians are in strength, dexterity, and subtlety. But when it comes to armies they do not bear comparison, and this springs entirely from the insufficiency of the leaders, since those who are capable are not obedient, and each one seems to himself to know, there having never been any one so distinguished above the rest, either by valour or fortune, that others would yield to him. Hence it is that for so long a time, and during so much fighting in the past twenty years, whenever there has been an army wholly Italian, it has always given a poor account of itself; the first witness to this is Il Taro, afterwards Allesandria, Capua, Genoa, Vaila, Bologna, and Mestri.

If, therefore, your illustrious house wishes to follow these remarkable men who have redeemed their country, it is necessary before all things, as a true foundation for every enterprise, to be provided with your own forces, because there can be no more faithful, truer, or better soldiers. And although singly they are good, altogether they will be much better when they find themselves commanded by their prince, honored by him, and maintained at his expense. Therefore it is necessary to be prepared with such arms, so that you can be defended against foreigners by Italian valour.

And although Swiss and Spanish infantry may be considered very formidable, nevertheless there is a defect in both, by reason of which a third order would not only be able to oppose them, but might be relied upon to overthrow them. For the Spaniards cannot resist cavalry, and the Switzers are afraid of infantry whenever they encounter them in close combat. Owing to this, as has been and may again be seen, the Spaniards are unable to resist French cavalry, and the Switzers are overthrown by Spanish infantry. And although a complete proof of this latter cannot be shown, nevertheless there was some evidence of it at the battle of Ravenna, when the Spanish infantry were confronted by German battalions, who follow the same tactics as the Swiss; when the Spaniards, by agility of body and with the aid of their shields, got in under the pikes of the Germans and stood out of danger, able to attack, while the Germans stood helpless, and, if the cavalry had not dashed up, all would have been over with them. It is possible, therefore, knowing the defects of both these infantries, to invent a new one, which will resist cavalry and not be afraid of infantry; this need not create a new order of arms, but a variation upon the old. And these are the kind of improvements which confer reputation and power upon a new prince.

This opportunity, therefore, ought not to be allowed to pass for letting Italy at last see her liberator appear. Nor can one express the love with which he would be received in all those provinces which have suffered so much from these foreign scourings, with what thirst for revenge, with what stubborn faith, with what devotion, with what tears. What door would be closed to him? Who would refuse obedience to him? What envy would hinder him? What Italian would refuse him homage? To all of us this barbarous dominion stinks.

Let, therefore, your illustrious house take up this charge with that courage and hope with which all just enterprises are undertaken, so that under its standard our native country may be ennobled.

Frederick the Great's Instructions to His Generals

ARTICLE I.

Of Prussian Troops, Their Excellencies, and Their Defects

The strictest care and the most unremitting attention are required of commanding officers in the formation of my troops. The most exact discipline is ever to be maintained, and the greatest regard paid to their welfare; they ought also to be better fed than almost any troops in Europe.

Our regiments are composed of half our own people and half foreigners who enlist for money: the latter only wait for a favorable opportunity to quit a service to which they have no particular attachment. The prevention of desertion therefore becomes an object of importance.

Many of our generals regard one man as good in effect as another, and imagine that if the vacancy be filled up, this man has no influence on the whole; but one does not know how on this subject to make a proper application of other armies to our own.

If a deserter be replaced by a man as well trained and disciplined as himself, it is a matter of no consequence; but if a soldier, who for two years has been accustomed to arms and military exercise, should desert, and be replaced by a bad subject, or perhaps none at all, the consequence must prove eventually very material.

It has happened from the negligence of officers in this particular, that regiments have not only been lessened in number, but that they have also lost their reputation.

By accidents of this kind, the army becomes weakened at the very period when its completion is most essentially necessary, and unless the greatest attention is paid to the circumstance, you will lose the best of your forces and never be able to recover yourself.

Though my country be well peopled, it is doubtful if many men are to be met with of the height of my soldiers: and supposing ever that there was no want of them, could they be disciplined in an instant? It therefore becomes one of the most essential duties of generals who command armies or detachments, to prevent desertion. This is to be effected,

1st. By not encamping too near a wood or forest, unless sufficient reason require it.

2dly. By calling the roll frequently every day.

3dly. By often sending out patrols of hussars, to scour the country round about the camp.

4thly. By placing chasseurs in the corn by night, and doubling the cavalry posts at dusk to strengthen the chain.

5thly. By not allowing the soldiers to wander about, and taking care that each troop be led regularly to water and forage by an officer.

6thly. By punishing all marauding with severity, as it gives rise to every species of disorder and irregularity.

7thly. By not drawing in the guards, who are placed in the villages on marching days, until the troops are under arms.

8thly. By forbidding, under the strictest injunctions, that any soldier on a march quit his rank or his division.

9thly. By avoiding night marches, unless obliged by necessity.

10thly. By pushing forward patrols of hussars to the right and left, whilst the infantry are passing through a wood.

11thly. By placing officers at each end of a defile, to oblige the soldiers to fall into their proper places.

12thly. By concealing from the soldier any retrograde movement which you may be obliged to make, or giving some specious flattering pretext for doing so.

13thly. By paying great attention to the regular issue of necessary subsistence, and taking care that the troops be furnished with bread, flesh, beer, brandy, etc.

14thly. By searching for the cause of the evil, when desertion shall have crept into a regiment or company: inquiring if the soldier has received his bounty and other customary indulgencies, and if there has been no misconduct on the part of the captain. No relaxation of discipline is however on any account to be permitted. It may be said that the colonel will take care of this business, but his efforts alone cannot be sufficient; for in an army, every individual part of it should aim at perfection, to make it appear to be the work of only one man.

An army is composed for the most part of idle and inactive men and unless the general has a constant eye upon them, and obliges them to do their duty, this artificial machine, which with the greatest care cannot be made perfect, will very soon fall to pieces, and nothing but the bare idea of a disciplined army will remain.

Constant employment for the troops is therefore indispensably necessary: the experience of officers who adopt such a plan will convince them of its good effects, and they will also perceive that there are daily abuses to be corrected, which pass unobserved by those who are too indolent to endeavor to discover them.

This constant and painful attention may appear at first sight as rather a hardship on the general, but its consequences will make him ample amends. With troops so fine, so brave, and so well disciplined, what advantage can he not obtain? A general, who with other nations would be regarded as being rash or half mad, would with us be only acting by established rules. Any enterprise which man is capable of executing, may be undertaken by him. Besides this, the soldiers will not suffer a man to remain amongst them who has betrayed any symptoms of shyness, which would certainly not be regarded in other armies.

I have been an eyewitness to the conduct both of officers and private soldiers, who could not be prevailed on, though dangerously wounded, to quit their post, or fall into the rear to get themselves dressed. With troops like these the world itself might be subdued, if conquests were not as fatal to the victors as to the vanquished. Let them be but well supplied with provisions, and you may attempt any thing with them. On a march you prevent the enemy by speed; at an attack of a wood, you will force them; if you make them climb a mountain, you will soon disperse those who make any resistance, and it then becomes an absolute massacre. If you put your cavalry into action, they will charge through the enemy at the sword's point and demolish them.

But as it is not alone sufficient that the troops be good, and as the ignorance of a general may be the means of losing every advantage, I shall proceed to speak of the qualities which a general ought to possess, and lay down such rules as I have either learned from well-informed generals, or purchased dearly by my own experience.

ARTICLE II.

Of the Subsistence of Troops, and of Provisions

It has been said by a certain general, that the first object in the establishment of an army ought to be making provision for the belly, that being the basis and foundation of all operations. I shall divide this subject into two parts: in the first I shall explain how and where magazines ought to be established, and in the latter, the method of employing, and transporting them.

The first rule is to establish the large magazines invariably in the rear of the army, and, if possible, in a place that is well secured. During the wars in Silesia and Bohemia, our grand magazine was at Breslau, on account of the advantage of being able to replenish it by means of the Oder. When magazines are formed at the head of an army, the first check may oblige you to abandon them, and you may be left without resource; whereas, if they are established in the rear of each other, the war will be prudently carried on, and one small disaster will not complete your ruin.

Spandau and Magdebourg should be the chosen situations for magazines in the frontier of the electorate. Magdebourg, on account of the Elbe, will be particularly serviceable in an offensive war against Saxony, and Schweidenitz against Bohemia.

You cannot be too cautious in the choice of commissaries and their deputies, for if they prove dishonest, the state will be materially injured. With this view, men of strict honor should be appointed as superiors, who must personally, frequently, and minutely examine and control the accounts.

There are two ways of forming magazines, either by ordering the nobility and peasants to bring their grain to the depot, and paying them for it according to the rate laid down by the chamber of finance, or by taking a certain quantity from them by requisition. It is the business of the commissary to settle and to sign all these agreements.

Vessels of a particular construction are built for the purpose of conveying corn and forage along the canals and rivers.

Purveyors are never to be employed but in cases of the last necessity, for even Jews [sic] are less exorbitant in their demands: they increase the price of provisions, and sell them out again at a most extravagant profit.

The magazines should be established at a very early period, that no kind of necessary may be wanting when the army leaves its quarters to begin a campaign: if they be too long neglected, the frost will put a stop to water carriage, or the roads will become so excessively deep and heavy, that their formation will be a business of the utmost difficulty.

Besides the regimental covered wagons which carry bread for eight days, the commissary is provided with conveniences for carrying provisions for a month.

The advantage of navigation is, however, never to be neglected, for without this convenience, no army can ever be abundantly supplied.

The wagons should be drawn by horses: trial has been made of oxen, but they do not answer the purpose.

The wagon masters must be exceedingly careful that due attention be paid to their cattle. The general of an army must also have an eye to this circumstance, for the loss of horses will necessarily occasion a diminution of wagons, and consequently of provisions.

Moreover, unless they receive a proper

quantity of good food, these horses will be unable to undergo the necessary fatigue. On a march, therefore, not only the horses will be lost, but also the wagons and their contents. The best concerted measures may be ruined by a repetition of such disasters. the general, therefore, must not neglect any of these circumstances, which are so materially important in all his operations.

In order to facilitate the carriage of provisions in a war against Saxony, advantage must be taken of the Elbe, and in Silesia of the Oder. The sea affords you this assistance in Prussia, but in Bohemia and Moravia, your only dependence is on carriages. It sometimes happens that three or four depots of provisions are formed on the same line, as was the case with us in Bohemia in the year 1742. There was a magazine at Pardubitz, at Nienbourg, at Podjebrod, and at Brandies, to enable us to keep pace with the enemy, and follow him to Prague, if he had thought proper to have gone thither.

During the last campaign in Bohemia, Breslau furnished Schweidenitz, Schweidenitz supplied Jaromirez, and from thence provisions were carried to the army.

Besides the covered wagons which carry provisions, iron ovens always travel with the army, (the number of which has of late been very much augmented), and, on every halting day, they are set to bake bread. On all expeditions, you should be supplied with bread or biscuit for ten days. A biscuit is a very good article, but our soldiers like it only in soup, nor do they know how to employ it to the best advantage.

On a march through an enemy's country, the depot of meal should ever be in a garrisoned town near the army. During the campaign of 1745, our depot was first at Neustadt, then at Jaromirez, and last at Trautenau. Had we been farther advanced, we could not have had a depot in security nearer than that at Pardubitz.

I have provided handmills for each company, which are found to be exceedingly useful, as they are worked by the soldiers, who carry the meal to the depot, and receive bread in return. With this meal, you are enabled to husband your magazines, and have it in your power to remain much longer in camp than you could without such supply. Moreover, fewer escorts, and a smaller number of convoys will also be found sufficient.

On the subject of convoys, I must enlarge a little. The strength of escorts depends on the fear which you entertain of the enemy. Detachments of infantry are sent into the towns through which the convoy will pass, to afford then a point of support. Large detachments to cover them are sometimes sent out, as was the case in Bohemia.

In all chequered countries, convoys should be escorted by the infantry, to which a few hussars may be added, in order to keep a lookout on the march, and inform themselves of all situations where the enemy may lie concealed.

My escorts have been formed of infantry in preference to cavalry even in a plain country, and in my own opinion, with very much advantage.

For what regards the minutiae of escorts, I refer you to my military regulation. The general of an army cannot be too anxious about the security of his convoys.

One good rule to attain this end is to send troops forward for the purpose of occupying the defiles through which the convoy is to pass, and to push the escort a league in front towards the enemy. By this maneuver the convoys are masked, and arrive in security.

ARTICLE III.

Of Sutlers, Beer, and Brandy

When you have it in contemplation to make any enterprise on the enemy, the commissary must be ordered to get together all the beer and brandy that he can lay his hands on, that the army may not want these articles, at least for the first days. As soon as the army enters an enemy's country, all the brewers and distillers who are in the neighborhood must immediately be put in requisition: the distillers, in particular, must be instantly set to work, that the soldier may not lose his dram, which he can very badly spare.

Protection must be afforded to the sutlers, especially in a country whose inhabitants are fled, and where provisions cannot be had for money. At such a time we are justified in not being over nice with respect to the peasantry.

The sutlers and women must be sent out in search of vegetables and cattle. The price of provisions is however, a matter that requires much attention, as the soldier ought to be allowed to purchase at a reasonable price, and at the same time the sutler should derive an honest profit.

It may here be added, that the soldier receives gratis during a campaign two pounds of bread per day, and two pounds of flesh per week. It is an indulgence which the poor fellows richly deserve, especially in Bohemia, where the country is but little better than a desert.

Convoys for the army should ever be followed by herds of cattle, for the support and nourishment of the soldier.

ARTICLE IV.

Of Dry and Green Forage

Oats, barley, hay, chopped straw, &c. compose what is called dry forage, and are carried to the magazine. If the oats be either fusty or moldy, the horses will contract the mange and farcy [a skin disease], and be so weakened as to be unserviceable even at the beginning of a campaign. Chopped straw is given because it is the custom, though it serves but barely to fill the belly.

The first object in collecting forage and carrying it to the magazine is either to get the start of the enemy at the opening of a campaign or to be prepared for some distant enterprise. But an army can seldom venture to move far from its magazines, as long as the horses are obliged to live on dry forage, on account of the inconvenience of moving it, as a whole province is sometimes unable to furnish a sufficient number of carriages. And in general, these are not the methods that we employ in an offensive war, unless there are no rivers, by means of which the forage can be transported.

During the campaign in Silesia, all my cavalry lived on dry forage, but we only marched from Strehla to Schwiedenitz (where there was a magazine,) and from thence to Cracau, where we were in the neighborhood of the Brieg and the Oder.

When any enterprise is about to take place in the winter, the cavalry should carry with them forage for five days well bound together on their horses, if Bohemia or Moravia are to be the scene of action, unless you mean to destroy all your cavalry. We forage in the fields for corn and vegetables as long as any remain there, and after the harvest in the villages.

When we encamp on a spot where we mean to make some stay, an account should be taken of the forage; and when its quantity be ascertained, a regular distribution of it should be made according to the number of days which we intend to remain.

All large foraging parties are escorted by a body of cavalry, the strength of which is proportioned to the vicinity of the enemy, and the fear which you entertain of him. Foraging is sometimes carried on by the wings, or even the whole of an army.

The foragers always assemble on the road which they intend taking, either on the wings, in front, or in the rear of the army.

The advance guard is composed of hussars, who are followed by the cavalry in a plain country, but in irregular situations, the infantry go before them. The advance guard is to precede the march of about a fourth part of the foragers, who are to be followed by a detachment of the escort, partly horse and partly foot; then another party of foragers, followed by a detachment of troops, and after them the remainder in the same order. the march of the rear guard so to be closed by a troop of hussars, who will form the rear of the whole column.

It is to be remembered, that in all escorts the infantry take their cannon with them, and the foragers their swords and carbines.

When arrived at the spot where they intend foraging, a chain is to be formed, and the infantry posted near the villages, behind the hedges, and in the hollow ways. Troops of cavalry joined with infantry should be formed into a reserve, and placed in the centre to be ready to support any point where the enemy may endeavor to make an impression. The hussars are to skirmish with the enemy, in order to amuse them and draw them off from the forage. As soon as the enclosure is complete, the foragers divide the ground by regiments. Great care must be taken by the officers commanding, that the trusses be made very large, and bound well together.

When the horses are laden, the foragers are to return to camp by troops, protected by small escorts, and as soon as they have all left the ground, the troops of the chain are to assemble and form the rear guard, followed by the hussars.

The method of foraging in villages differs from the foregoing only in this instance, viz. the infantry are posted round the village, and the cavalry behind them in a situation where they may be able to act. Villages are to be foraged one by one, to prevent the troops of the chain from being too much dispersed.

In mountainous countries, foraging becomes an arduous business, and on such occasions the greatest part of the escorts must be composed of infantry and hussars.

When we are encamped near the enemy, and intend remaining there some time, we must endeavor to secure the forage which is between the two camps. After that, we are to forage for two leagues round, beginning with the most distant fields, and preserving those that are near home till the last. If no stay be intended, we forage in the camp and in the neighborhood.

When it becomes an object to secure a large quantity of green forage, I would rather send the parties out twice, than occupy too great an extent of country at once. By this means you will preserve your chain more snug and compact, and the foragers will be in much greater security: whereas if too great a space be occupied, the chain must consequently be weakened and rendered liable to be forced.

ARTICLE V.

Of the Knowledge of a Country

The knowledge of a country is to be attained in two ways; the first (and that with which we ought to begin) is by a careful and studious examination of a map of the country which is intended to be the scene of war, and by marking on it very distinctly the names of all the rivers, towns, and mountains that are of any consequence.

Having by this means gained a general idea of the country, we must proceed to a more particular and minute examination of it, to inform ourselves of the directions of the high roads, the situation of the towns, whether by a little trouble they can be made tenable, on what side to attack them if they are possessed by the enemy, and what number of troops are necessary for their defense.

We should also be provided with plans of the fortified towns, that we may be acquainted with their strength, and what are their most assailable parts. The course and depth of the large rivers should also be ascertained, how far they are navigable, and if shallow enough at any points to allow of being forded. It should also be known what rivers are impassible in spring and dry in summer. This sort of inquiry must extend likewise to the marshes of any consequence that may be in the country.

In a flat, smooth country, the fertile parts should be distinguished from those that are not so, and we must be well acquainted with all the marches that either the enemy or ourselves can undertake, to pass from one great city or river to another. It will be necessary also to break up those camps, which are liable to be taken on that route.

A flat, open country can be reconnoitered presently, but the view is so confined in that which is woody and mountainous, that it becomes a business of much difficulty.

In order, therefore, to procure intelligence so highly important, we must ascend the heights, taking the map with us, and also some of the elders of the neighboring villages, such as huntsmen and shepherds. If there be one mountain higher than another, that must be ascended, to gain an idea of a country which we wish to discover.

We must gain a knowledge of the roads, not only to be satisfied in how many columns we may march, but also that we may be enabled to plan a variety of projects, and be informed how we may reach the enemy's camp and force it, should any be established in the neighborhood, or how to place ourselves on his flank, should he alter his position.

One of the most material objects is to reconnoiter situations that, in case of necessity, may serve as camps of defense, as well as a field of battle, and the posts that may be occupied by the enemy.

A just idea must be formed of all these matters of intelligence, as well as of the most considerable posts, the valleys, chief defiles, and all the advantageous situations which the country affords, and we must seriously reflect on every operation that may take place, so that by being prepared beforehand with a plan of arrangements, we may not be embarrassed when called into action. These reflections should be well connected, and maturely digested, with all the care and patience that an object of so much consequence requires; and unless we can arrange the matter to our satisfaction the first time, we must try it over again and again till we have got it perfect.

It is a general rule in the choice of all camps, whether for offense or defense, that both wood and water be near at hand, that the front be close and well covered, and the rear perfectly open.

If circumstances forbid the examination of a country in the manner laid down, clever, intelligent officers should be sent thither under any kind of excuse, or even in disguise if necessary. They are to be well informed of the nature of the observations which they are to make, and at their return, the remarks which they have made on the camps and different situations are to be noted on a map: but when we can make use of our own eyes, we ought never to trust those of other people.

ARTICLE VI.

Of the Coup D'Oeil

The coup d'oeil may be reduced, properly speaking, to two points; the first of which is having the abilitiy to judge how many troops a certain extent of country can contain. This talent can only be acquired by practice, for after having laid out several camps, the eye will gain so exact an idea of space, that you will seldom make any material mistake in your calculations.

The other, and by far the most material point, is to be able to distinguish at first sight all the advantages of which any given space of ground is capable. This art is to be acquired and even brought to perfection, though a man be not absolutely born with a military genius.

Fortification, as it possesses rules that are applicable to all situations of an army, is undoubtedly the basis and foundation of this coup d'oeil. Every defile, marsh, hollow way, and even the smallest eminence, will be converted by a skillful general to some advantage.

Two hundred different positions may sometimes be taken up in the space of two square leagues, of which an intelligent general knows how to select that which is the most advantageous. In the first place, he will ascend even the smallest eminences to discover and reconnoiter the ground; and assisted by the same rules of fortification, he will be enabled to find out the weak part of the enemy's order of battle. If time permits, the general would do well to pace over the ground, when he has determined on his general position.

Many other advantages may also be derived from the same rules of fortification, such as, the manner of occupying heights, and how to choose them, that they may not be commanded by others; in what manner the wings are to be supported, that the flanks may be well covered; how to take up positions that may be defended, and avoid those which a man of reputation cannot, without great risk, maintain. These rules will also enable him to discover where the enemy is weakest, either by having taken an unfavorable position, distributed his force without judgment, or from the slender means of defense which he derives from his situation. I am led by these reflections to explain in what manner troops ought to be distributed so as to make the most of their ground.

ARTICLE VII.

Of the Distribution of Troops

Though the knowledge and choice of ground are very essential points, it is of no less importance that we know how to profit by such advantages, so that the troops may be placed in situations that are proper and convenient for them.

Our cavalry, being designed to act with velocity, can only be made use of on a plain, whereas the infantry may be employed in every possible variety of ground. Their fire is for defense, and their bayonet for attack. We always begin by the defensive, as much caution is necessary for the security of a camp, where the vicinity of the enemy may at any moment bring on an engagement.

The greater part of the orders of battle now existing are of ancient date: we tread in the steps of our ancestors without regulating matters according to the nature of the ground, and hence it is that a false and erroneous application so often takes place.

The whole of an army should be placed in order of battle agreeably to the nature of ground which every particular part of it requires. The plain is chosen for the cavalry, but this is not all which regards them; for if the plain be only a thousand yards in front, and bounded by a wood in which we suppose the enemy to have thrown some infantry, under whose fire their cavalry can rally, it will then become necessary to change the disposition, and place them at the extremities of the wings of the infantry, that they may receive the benefit of their support.

The whole of the cavalry is sometimes placed on one of the wings, or in the second line; at other times, their wings are closed by one or two brigades of infantry.

Eminences, churchyards, hollow ways, and wide ditches are the most advantageous situations for an army. If, in the disposition of our troops, we know how to take advantage of these circumstances, we never need to fear being attacked.

If your cavalry be posted with a morass in its front, it is impossible that it can render you any service: and if it be placed too near a wood, the enemy may have troops there, who may throw them into disorder and pick them off with their muskets, whilst they are deprived of every possible means of defense. Your infantry will be exposed to the same inconveniencies if they are advanced too far on a plain with their flanks not secured, for the enemy will certainly take advantage of such error, and make their attack on that side where they are unprotected.

The nature of the ground must invariably be our rule of direction. In a mountainous country I should place my cavalry in the second line, and never use them in the first line except they could act to advantage, unless it be a few squadrons to fall on the flank of the enemy's infantry who may be advancing to attack me.

It is a general rule in all well-disciplined armies, that a reserve of cavalry be formed if we are on a plain, but where the country is chequered and intersected, this reserve is formed of infantry, with the addition of some hussars and dragoons.

The great art of distributing troops on the field is to place them so that all have room to act and be uniformly useful. Villeroi, who perhaps was not well acquainted with this rule, deprived himself of the assistance of the whole of his left wing on the plain of Ramillies, by having posted them behind a morass, where it was morally impossible that they could maneuvre, or render any sort of support to his right wing.

ARTICLE VIII.

Of Camps

To be convinced that your camp be well chosen, you must discover whether a trifling movement of yours will oblige the enemy to make one of greater consequence, or, if after one march, he be under the necessity of making others. They who have the least occasion to move, are certainly the best situated.

The choice of situation for a camp should rest entirely with the general of an army, as it often becomes the field of battle, and the success of his enterprises so materially depends upon it.

As there are many observations to be made on this subject, I shall enter into it very particularly, saying nothing with respect to the method of placing troops in camp, but referring you on that head to my military regulation.

I now proceed to speak only of affairs of consequence, and of matters that more immediately concern the general himself.

All camps are designed to answer two purposes, defense and attack. The first class consists of those camps in which an army assembles where the sole object is the convenience and accommodation of the troops. They ought to be encamped in small bodies near the magazine, but so situated that they may readily be assembled in order of battle.

Camps of this kind are generally formed at such distance from the enemy as to be free from all alarm. The king of England, who neglected this caution, and imprudently encamped himself on the bank of the Mein opposite the French army, ran a very great risk of being defeated at Dettinghen.

The first rule to be observed in the marking out of a camp is that both wood and water be at no great distance.

It is our custom to entrench camps, in the manner of the Romans, not only to secure ourselves against any enterprise which the numerous light troops of the enemy may attempt against us, but also to prevent desertion.

I have constantly observed that fewer men have left us when the redans [a fleche, or angular entrenchment, like an arrow] were joined by two lines that extended all round the camp, than when this caution has been neglected. This is a serious fact, however ridiculous or trifling it may appear.

Camps of repose are those where we expect

forage; on some occasions they are designed to watch the enemy, who have as yet made no movements, that we may be regulated by their maneuvers. As relaxation is the only object in camps of this nature, they should be rendered secure by being in the rear of a large river or morass, or in short by any means that will render their front inaccessible. Of this description was our camp at Strehla.

If the brooks and rivers in front of the camp are too shallow, dams must be employed in order to deepen them.

Though there be no dread of the enemy to annoy us in camps of this kind, the general of an army must nevertheless on no account be idle. The leisure which he now has must be employed in paying attention to the troops, and reestablishing the usual discipline. He must examine if the service be carried on in strict conformity to order, if the officers on guard are attentive and well informed of the duties of their situation, and if the rules which I have laid down for the posting of cavalry and infantry guards be properly and strictly observed.

The infantry should go through their exercise three times a week, and the recruits once every day: on some occasions also entire corps may perform their maneuvers together. The cavalry must likewise go through their evolutions, unless they are employed in foraging; and the general, knowing the exact strength of each corps, should take particular care that the recruits and young horses be well drilled. He must also frequently visit the lines, commending those officers who pay attention to their troops, and severely rebuking those who appear to have neglected them, for it is not to be supposed that a large army can be self-animated. It will ever abound with idlers and malingerers, who require the general's attention to be put in motion and be obliged to do their duty.

Very great utility will be derived from camps of this sort, if they be employed in the manner which I have recommended, and the succeeding campaign will prove the good effects of their discipline and order.

We form our encampment, or we forage, near to the enemy, or at a considerable distance from him—I shall only speak of the former, where it is necessary that we make choice of the most fertile spots, and encamp in a situation which art or nature has rendered formidable.

When foraging camps are situated near the enemy, they should be very difficult of access, as foraging parties are regarded as detachments sent out against the enemy.

These parties may consist of a sixth part, or even half, of an army. It would afford fine amusement to the enemy, if they were able on these occasions to attack us to our disadvantage, and it would certainly happen, but for the wellchosen situation of our camp.

But though the position be very good, and apparently there be nothing to fear from the enemy, there are, notwithstanding, other cautions which are by no means to be neglected. The most rigid secrecy must be observed both in regard to the time and place of foraging, nor should even the general who is to command on the occasion be acquainted with these circumstances till a late hour in the preceding evening.

We should send out as many detached parties as possible, to be more certainly informed of any movements which the enemy may make: and unless prevented by reasons that are very material, we may, to save trouble, forage on the same day that they do. We are not, however, to place too much confidence in this circumstance, as the enemy, by being apprised of our design, may countermand the order for foraging, and attack the main body.

The camp of Prince Charles of Lorraine under Konigingraetz was inaccessible by nature, and extremely convenient for the purposes of foraging.

That which we occupied at Cholm was made strong by art, viz. by the abbatis [a defensive obstacle formed by felled trees with sharpened branches facing the enemy] which I ordered to be thrown up on our right wing and the redoubts which were in front of the infantry camp.

We entrenched a camp, when it is our intention to lay siege to a place, to defend a difficult pass, and supply the defects of the situation by throwing up works so as to be secure from every insult on the part of the enemy.

The rules which a general has to observe in the formation of all entrenchments are, to take advantage of every marsh, river, inundation, and abbatis which may serve to render the extent of his entrenchments more difficult. They had better be too small than too large, for the progress of the enemy is not checked by the entrenchments themselves, but by the troops who defend them.

I would not wish to make entrenchments, unless I could line them with a chain of battalions, and had also at my disposal a reserve of infantry that could be moved to any point as occasion might require. Abbatis are no longer of service than whilst they are defended by infantry.

The chief attention should be paid to the proper support of the lines of countervallation, which generally end in a river; and in such case the fosse should be carried some length into the river, and be so deepened as not to allow it being forded. If this precaution be neglected, you run the hazard of having your flank turned. It is necessary that you be abundantly supplied with provisions before you sit down behind the lines to besiege any place.

The flanks of entrenchments should be particularly strong, nor should there be a single point which the enemy might attack without being exposed to four or five crossfires. Infinite care and caution are required in the formation of entrenchments which are designed to defend the passes and defiles of mountains. The support of the flanks is here most essentially necessary, to accomplish which, redoubts are formed on the two wings: sometimes the whole entrenchment itself is made up of redoubts, so that the troops who defend it are in no danger of being turned.

Intelligent generals are well informed on how to oblige the enemy to attack those points where the work is made strongest by the ditch being widened, deepened, and lined with pallisades, chevaux-de-frize [defenses consisting of lumber or iron barrels covered with projecting spikes and often strung with barbed wire] placed at the entrances, the parapet made cannonproof, and pits dug in the places that are most exposed.

But for the covering of a siege, I would always prefer an army of observation to an entrenched camp, and for this plain reason, because we are taught by experience that the old method is not to be depended on.

The Prince of Conde saw his entrenchment which was before Arras forced by Turenne, and Conde (if I am not mistaken) forced that which Turenne had formed before Valenciennes—since that period, neither of these great masters in the military art have made any use of them, but, to cover a siege, have always employed armies of observation.

I shall now treat of defensive camps, which are only strong by situation, and intended solely to be secure from the attacks of the enemy.

To render these situations equal to the purposes for which they are designed, it is necessary, that the front and both flanks be of equal strength, and the rear perfectly free and open. Of such nature are those heights, whose front is very extensive, and whose flanks are covered by marshes, as was the camp of Prince Charles of Lorraine at Marschwitz, where the front was covered by a marshy river, and the flanks by lakes; or like that which we occupied at Konopist in the year 1744.

We may also shelter ourselves under the

protection of some fortified place, as was done by the Marshal de Neipperg, who after being defeated at Mollwitz, took up an excellent position under the walls of Neiss. As long as a general can maintain his post in camps of this kind, he will be secure from attack; but as soon as the enemy is in motion with a view of turning him, he will no longer be able to remain. His arrangements should therefore be so settled beforehand, that if the enemy succeed in their attempt to turn him, he may have nothing to do but fall back, and take up another strong position in the rear.

Bohemia abounds in camps of this description, and as the country is so chequered by nature, we are often obliged to occupy some of them against our inclination.

I must again repeat how necessary it is for a general to be on his guard, lest he be led, by a bad choice of posts, into errors that cannot be remedied, or in a situation from which he has no means of escaping but by a narrow defile. For if he have a clever enemy to deal with, he will be so closely pent up, and so completely prevented from fighting by the nature of the ground, as to be obliged to submit to the greatest indignity which a soldier can suffer, that of laying down his arms without the power of defending himself.

In camps that are intended to cover a country, the strength of the place itself is not the object of attention, but those points which are liable to attack, and by means of which the enemy may penetrate. These should all be surrounded by the camp. Not that it is necessary to occupy every opening by which the enemy may advance upon us, but that one only which would lead to his desired point, and that situation which affords us security, and from which we have it in our power to alarm him. In short, we should occupy that post, which will oblige the enemy to take circuitous routes, and enable us, by small movements, to disconcert his projects.

The camp at Neustadt defends the whole of Lower Silesia against the attacks of an army that may be in Moravia. The proper position to take up, is to have the city of Neustadt and the river in front, and if the enemy shows a design to pass between Ottmachau and Glatz, we have only to move between Neiss and Ziegenhals, and there take up an advantageous camp which will cut them off from Moravia.

For the same reason the enemy will not dare to stir on the side of Cosel, for by placing myself between Troppau and Jaegerndorff (where there are many very excellent positions) I cut him off from his convoys.

There is another camp of equal importance between Liebau and Schaemberg, which secures all Lower Silesia against Bohemia.

In all these positions, the rules which I have laid down ought to be observed, as far as circumstances will allow. I must yet add one more, which is that when you have a river in front, you never allow tents to be pitched on the ground which you intend for the field of battle at a greater distance than half a musketshot from the front of the camp.

The frontier of the electorate of Brandenberg is a country which no camp can cover, as it has six leagues of plain ground which is open the whole way. To defend it against Saxony, it is necessary to be possessed of Wittenberg, and either encamp there or adopt the plan of the expedition which took place there in the winter of the year 1745. The camp at Werben covers and defends all that part which is on the side of the country of Hanover.

The front and flanks of a camp for offense must be always closed; for unless the flanks, which are the weakest part of an army, are well closed, you have nothing to expect from your troops. This was the fault of our camp at Czaslaw, before the battle of the year 1742.

The village houses which are on the wings, or

in the front of our camp, are always occupied by troops, except on fighting days, when they are called in, lest by the enemy's setting fire to such badlyconstructed wooden buildings (as our own cottages and those of our neighbors generally are) the men may also be destroyed. There may, however, be an exception to this general rule, when any stone houses are in the villages, or any churchyards which do not communicate with wooden buildings.

But as it is our constant principle to attack, and not act on the defensive, this kind of post should never be occupied except it be at the head of the army, or in front of its wings; in such situations it will afford much protection to our troops in the attack, and prove of great annoyance to the enemy during the action.

It is also a circumstance of material import, that the depth of the small rivers or marshes which are in front or on the flanks of our camp be well ascertained, lest by the rivers being fordable, or the marshes practicable, you discover too late that you have trusted to a false point of defense.

Villars was beaten at Malplaquet by conceiving that the marsh on his right was impracticable, which proved to be only a dry meadow, which our troops passed to take him in the flank. Every thing should be examined by our own eyes, and no attentions of this nature treated on any account as matters of indifference.

ARTICLE IX.

How to Secure a Camp

The front of the first line must be defended by the regiments of infantry, and if a river be there, piquets [pickets] must be posted on its banks. The rear of the camp is to be guarded by piquets from the second line. These piquets are to be covered by redans, joined by slight entrenchments, by means of which the camp will be entrenched after the manner of the Romans. We must occupy the villages which are on the wings, or even to the distance of half a league from thence, if they serve to defend any other passages.

The cavalry guards are to be posted agreeably to the rules laid down in my military regulation. We seldom had more than 300 maitres de garde [private dragoons on guard] amongst 80 squadrons, unless we were very near to the enemy, as when we marched to Schweidenitz between the battle of Hohen-Freidberg, and again when we marched into Lusatia in order to go to Naumbourg. These advance guards should be composed of all sorts of troops, for example, 2000 hussars, 1500 dragoons, and 2000 grenadiers. The general who has the command of bodies of men that are advanced, should be a man of sound understanding, and as it is his object to gain intelligence, not expose himself to action, his camps should be chosen with judgment, having in their front either woods or defiles with which he is well acquainted. He must also send out frequent patrols for the purpose of gaining information, that he may know at every instant what is going forward in the camp of the enemy.

If in the meantime you employ the hussars who remain with you to patrol in the rear and on the wings of the camp, you have taken all possible precautions to be guarded against any hostile enterprises.

Should a considerable body of troops endeavor to slide in between you and your rear guard, you may be assured that they have formed some design against it, and you are therefore to hasten to its support.

To conclude all that I have to say on this subject, it must be added, that if those generals who canton their troops wish to be free from danger and alarm, they should only occupy those villages which are between the two lines.

ARTICLE X.

In What Manner and for What Reason We Are to Send Out Detachments

It is only repeating an ancient maxim in war to say, "That he who divides his force will be beaten in detail." If you are about to give battle, strain every nerve to get together as many troops as you possibly can, for they never can be employed to better purpose. Almost every general who has neglected this rule, has found ample reason to repent of it.

Albemarle's detachment, which was beaten at Oudenarde, lost to the great Eugene the whole campaign; and General Stahrenberg was beaten at the battle of Villa Viciosa in Spain, by being separated from the English troops.

Detachments have also proved very fatal to the Austrians in the latter campaigns that they have made in Hungary. The Prince of Hildbourghausen was defeated at Banjaluka, and General Wallis suffered a check on the banks of the Timok. The Saxons also were beaten at

Kesseldorf, for want of having joined Prince
Charles, as they could have done. I should have
been defeated at Sohr, and deservedly too, if
presence of mind in my generals, and valor in my
troops, had not rescued me from such
misfortune. It may be asked, are we then never to
send out detachments? My reply is that it is a
business of so delicate a nature, as never to be
hazarded but on the most pressing necessity, and
for reasons of the utmost importance.

When you are acting offensively, detachments
ought never to be employed, and even though
you are in an open country, and have some
places in your possession, no more troops are to
be spared than are barely sufficient to secure
your convoys.

Whenever war is made in Bohemia or
Moravia, necessity requires that troops be sent out
to insure the arrival of provisions. Encampments
must be formed on the chain of mountains which
the convoys are obliged to pass, and remain there
till you have collected provisions for some
months, and are possessed of some strong place
in the enemy's country that will serve as a depot.

Whilst these troops are absent on
detachments, you are to occupy advantageous
camps, and wait for their return.

The advance guard is not reckoned as a

detachment, because it should ever be near the army, and not to venture on any account too near the enemy.

It sometimes happens, that when we are acting on the defensive, we are forced to make detachments. Those which I had in Upper Silesia were in perfect safety by confining themselves, as I have already observed, to the neighborhood of fortified places.

Officers who have the command of detachments, should be men of prudence and resolution, for though they receive general instructions from their chief, it remains for themselves to consult on the propriety of advancing or retreating, as occasion may require.

When the force of the opponents is too strong, they should fall back, but on the other hand, they should well know how to take advantage, if the superiority happens to be on their own sides.

If the enemy approach by night, they will sometimes retire, and whilst they are supposed to be put to flight, return briskly to the charge and defeat them.

No regard whatever is to be paid to the light troops.

The first thing to be attended to by an officer who commands a detachment is his own safety, and when that is secured, he is at liberty to form against the enemy. To ensure rest to he must keep his adversary constantly by continually contriving plans against him, and if he succeed in two or three instances, the enemy will be obliged to keep on the defensive.

If these detachments be near the army, they will establish a communication with it by means of some town or neighboring wood.

In a war of defense, we are naturally induced to make detachments. Generals of little experience are anxious to preserve every thing, whilst the man of intelligence and enterprise regards only the grand point, in hopes of being able to strike some great stroke, and suffers patiently a small evil that may secure him against one of more material consequence.

The army of the enemy should be the chief object of our attention, its designs must be discovered, and opposed as vigorously as possible. In the year 1745 we abandoned Upper Silesia to the ravages of the Hungarians, that we might be better enabled to thwart the intentions of Prince Charles of Lorraine, and we made no detachments until we had defeated his army. When that was done, General Nassau in fifteen days cleared the whole of Upper Silesia of the Hungarians.

It is a custom with some generals to detach troops when they are about to make an attack, to take the enemy in the rear during the action, but much danger attends a movement of this kind, as the detachments generally lose their road, and arrive either too early or too late. The detachment which Charles XII sent out on the evening before the battle of Pultawa lost its way, and was the cause of the army's being beaten. Prince Eugene's design of surprising Cremona failed also from the too late arrival of the detachment of the Prince of Vaudemont, which was intended to attack the gate of Po.

Detachments should never take place on the day of battle, unless it be in the manner of Turenne near Colmar, where he presented his first line to the army of the Elector Frederick William, whilst the second line passing through defiles attacked him in flank and routed him. Or we may copy the example of the Marshal de Luxembourg at the battle of Fleury, in the year 1690, who posted a body of infantry in some high corn on the Prince of Waldeck's flank, and by that maneuver gained the battle.

After a victory, but never till then, troops may be detached for the protection of convoys, but even in this case they should not proceed a greater length than half a league from the army.

I shall conclude this article by saying that detachments which weaken the army one half, or even a third part, are excessively dangerous, and strongly to be disapproved.

ARTICLE XI.

Of the Tricks and Stratagems of War

In War, the skin of a fox is at times as necessary as that of the lion, for cunning may succeed when force fails. Since, therefore, force may at one time be repelled by force, and at another be obliged to yield to stratagem, we ought to be well acquainted with the use of both, that we may on occasion adopt either.

I have no wish to recite here the almost infinite list of stratagems, for they have all the same end in view, which is to oblige the enemy to make unnecessary marches in favor of our own designs. Our real intentions are to be studiously concealed, and the enemy misled by our affecting plans which we have no wish to execute.

When our troops are on the point of assembling, we countermarch them in a variety of ways, to alarm the enemy, and conceal from him the spot where we really wish to assemble and force a passage.

If there be fortresses in the country, we choose to encamp in a situation that threatens three or four places at the same time. Should the enemy think proper to throw troops into all these places, the consequence will be, that his force will be so weakened, that we shall have a good opportunity of falling on him: but if one point only has been the object of his attention, we lay siege to that which is the most defenseless.

If the object be to pass a river, or be possessed of some post of importance, you must withdraw to a great distance both from the post and from the spot where you mean to pass, in order to entice the enemy after you. And when everything is arranged and your march concealed, you are to betake yourself suddenly to the settled point and possess yourself of it.

If you wish to come to an action, and the enemy seems disposed to avoid it, you must appear to be in dread of the force which is opposed to you, or spread a report that your army is much weakened. We played this game before the battle of Hohen-Friedburg. I caused all the roads to be repaired as if I meant, at the approach of Prince Charles, to march to Breslau in four columns: his self-confidence seconding my design, he followed me into the plain, and was defeated.

Sometimes we contract the dimensions of the camp, to give it the appearance of weakness, and send out small detachments, (that we affect to be of great consequence) in order that the enemy may hold us cheap, and neglect an opportunity which he might improve. In the campaign of 1745, if it had been my intention to take Konigingraetz and Pardubitz, I had only to make two marches through the country of Glatz on the side of Moravia, as that would certainly have alarmed Prince Charles and brought him thither, to defend the place from which, after leaving Bohemia, he drew all his provisions. You will be sure of creating jealousy in the enemy, if you threaten places that either communicate with the capital or serve as depots for his provisions.

If we have no inclination to fight, we put a bold face upon the business, and give out that we are much stronger than we really are. Austria is a famous school for this sort of maneuver, for with them the art is brought to its greatest perfection.

By keeping up a bold and determined appearance, you give the idea of wishing to engage, and occasion a report to be circulated that you are meditating some very bold and daring enterprise: by means of which the enemy, in dread of the consequences of an attack, will frequently remain on the defensive.

It is an essential object in a war of defense, to know how to make a good choice of posts, and to maintain them to the last extremity: when forced to retire, the second line begins to move, followed insensibly by the first, and as you have defiles in your front, the enemy will not be able to take advantage of you in the retreat.

Even during the retreat, the positions that are taken up should be so oblique as to keep the enemy as much as possible in the dark. The more he endeavors to discover your designs, the more he will be alarmed, whilst you indirectly obtain the object of your wishes.

Another stratagem of war is to show to the enemy a front of very great extent, and if he mistakes a false attack for a real one he will inevitably be defeated.

By means of tricks also, we oblige the enemy to send out detachments, and when they are marched, take the opportunity of falling on him.

The best stratagem is to lull the enemy into security at the time when the troops are about to disperse and go into winter quarters, so that by retiring, you may be enabled to advance on them to some good purpose. With the view, the troops should be so distributed, as to assemble again very readily, in order to force the enemy's quarters. If this measure succeed, you may recover in a fortnight the misfortunes of a whole campaign.

Peruse with attention the two last campaigns of Turenne, for they are the chefs d'oeuvres of the stratagems of this age.

The schemes which our ancestors employed in war are now only in use amongst the light troops, whose practice it is to form ambuscades, and endeavor by a pretended flight to draw the enemy into a defile, that they may cut them in pieces. The generals of the present day seldom manage their matters so badly as to be taken in by such contrivances. Nevertheless, Charles XII was betrayed at Pultawa through the treachery of one of the Cossack chiefs. The same accident also befell Peter I on the Pruth, owing to the misconduct of a prince of that country. Both these men had promised a supply of provisions which it was not in their power to furnish.

As the method of making war by parties and detachments is fully laid down in my Military Regulation, I refer to that work all those who wish to refresh their memories, as it is a subject on which I have nothing further to advance.

To be informed of the method to oblige the enemy to make detachments, we have only to read over the glorious campaign of 1690, made by the Marshal de Luxembourg against the King of England, which concluded with the battle of Neerwinde.

ARTICLE XII.

Of Spies, How They Are to Be Employed On Every Occasion, and In What Manner We Are to Learn Intelligence of the Enemy

If we were acquainted beforehand with the intentions of the enemy, we should always be more than a match for him even with an inferior force. It is an advantage which all generals are anxious to procure, but very few obtain.

Spies may be divided into several classes: 1st, common people who choose to be employed in such concern; 2dly, double spies; 3dly, spies of consequence; 4thly, those who are compelled to take up the unpleasant business.

The common gentry, viz. peasants, mechanics, priests, &c. which are sent into the camp, can only be employed to discover where the enemy is: and their reports are generally so incongruous and obscure, as rather to increase our uncertainties than lessen them.

The intelligence of deserters is, for the most part, not much more to be depended on. A soldier knows very well what is going forward in his own regiment, but nothing farther. The hussars being detached in front, and absent the greatest part of their time from the army, are often ignorant on which side it is encamped. Nevertheless, their reports must be committed to paper, as the only means of turning them to any advantage.

Double spies are used to convey false intelligence to the enemy. There was an Italian at Schmiedeberg, who acted as a spy to the Austrians, and being told by us, that when the enemy approached we should retire to Breslau, he posted with the intelligence to Prince Charles of Lorraine, who narrowly escaped being taken in by it.

The post-master at Versailles was a long time in the pay of Prince Eugene. This unfortunate fellow opened the letters and orders which were sent from the court to the generals, and transmitted a copy of them to Prince Eugene, who generally received them much earlier than the commanders of the French army.

Luxembourg had gained over to his interest a secretary of the King of England, who informed him of all that passed. The king discovered it, and derived every advantage from it that could be expected in an affair of such delicacy: he obliged the traitor to write to Luxembourg, informing him that the allied army would be out the day following on a large foraging party. The consequence was that the French very narrowly escaped being surprised at Steinquerque, and would have been cut to pieces if they had not defended themselves with extraordinary valor. It would be very difficult to obtain such spies in a war against Austria: not that the Austrians are less alive to bribery than other people, but because their army is surrounded by such a cloud of light troops, who suffer no creature to pass without being well searched. This circumstance suggested to me the idea of bringing over some of their hussar officers, by means of whom a correspondence might be carried on in the following manner. It is a custom with hussars, when opposed to each other as skirmishing parties, to agree every now and then to a suspension of arms, which opportunity might be employed in conveying letters.

When we wish to gain intelligence of the enemy, or give him a false impression of our situation and circumstances, we employ a trusty soldier to go from our camp to that of the enemy, and report what we wish to have believed. He may also be made the bearer of handbills calculated to encourage desertion. Having completed his business, he may take a circuitous march and return to camp.

There is yet another way to gain intelligence of the enemy when milder methods fail, though I confess it to be a harsh and cruel practice. We find out a rich citizen who has a large family and good estate, and allow him a man who understands the language of the country dressed as a servant, whom we force him to take along with him into the enemy's camp, as his valet or coachman, under pretense of complaining of some injuries which he has received; he is to be threatened also at the same time, that if he does not return after a certain period, and bring the man with him, that his houses shall be burned, and his wife and children hacked in pieces. I was obliged to have recourse to this scheme at ... and it succeeded to my wish.

I must farther add, that in the payment of spies we ought to be generous, even to a degree of extravagance. That man certainly deserves to be well rewarded, who risks his neck to do your service.

ARTICLE XIII.

Of Certain Marks, By Which the Intentions of the Enemy Are To Be Discovered

The knowledge of the spot which the enemy has chosen as a depot for his provisions is the surest means of discovering his intentions before the campaign opens. For example, if the Austrians establish their magazines at Olmutz, we may be assured that they mean to attack Upper Silesia: if at Konigingraetz, we may be convinced that part of Schweidenitz is threatened. When it was the wish of the Saxons to invade the frontier of the Electorate, their magazines marked their intended route, for they were established at Zittau, Goerlitz, and at Guben, which are on the road leading to Crossen.

The first object of intelligence should be, on what side and in what situations the enemy means to fix his magazines.

The French played a double game, by forming depots on the Meuse and on the Scheld, in order to conceal their intentions.

When the Austrians are encamped, it is easy to discover when they intend moving, by their custom of cooking on the days of march. If, therefore, much smoke be perceived in their camp at five or six o'clock in the morning, you may take it for granted on that day they mean to move.

Whenever the Austrians intend fighting, all their strong detachments of light troops are called in; and when you have observed this, it behooves you to be very well upon your guard.

If you attack a post which is defended by their Hungarian troops, without being able to make any impression on it, you may be satisfied that the army is near at hand to support them.

If their light troops endeavor to post themselves between your army and the body of men which you have detached, you may be assured that the enemy has a design on that detachment, and your measures must be taken accordingly. It must be added, that if the same general be always opposed to you, his designs will be readily discovered, and his plan of conduct very soon become familiar.

After mature reflection on the nature of the

country which is the scene of war, the state of the army which you command, the safety of the magazines, the strength of the fortified places, the means which the enemy may be able to employ in order to gain possession of them, the mischief which the light troops may do by posting themselves on your flanks, rear, and other parts, or if the enemy should employ them to make a diversion; I say, after having well deliberated on all these points, you may conclude that an intelligent enemy will attempt that enterprise which is likely to give you the greatest annoyance, at least that such will be his intention, to frustrate which your every effort must be exerted.

ARTICLE XIV.

Of Our Own Country, and That Which is Either Neutral or Hostile; of the Variety of Religions, and of the Different Conduct Which Such Circumstances Require

War may be carried on in three different kinds of country: either in our own territories, those belonging to neutral powers, or in the country of an enemy.

If glory were my only object, I would never make war but in my own country, by reason of its manifold advantages, as every man there acts as a spy, nor can the enemy stir a foot without being betrayed.

Detachments of any strength may boldly be sent out, and may practice in safety all the maneuvers of which war is capable.

If the enemy have the advantage, every peasant turns soldier and lends a hand to annoy him, as was experienced by the Elector Frederick William after the battle of Fehrbelin, where a greater number of Swedes was destroyed by the peasants than fell in the engagement. After the battle of Hohen-Friedberg, also, I observed that the mountaineers in Silesia brought into us the runaway Austrians in great abundance.

When war is carried on in a neutral country, the advantage seems to be equal, and the object of attention then is to rival the enemy in the confidence and friendship of the inhabitants. To attain this end, the most exact discipline must be observed, marauding and every kind of plunder strictly forbidden, and its commission punished with exemplary severity. It may not be amiss also, to accuse the enemy of harboring some pernicious designs against the country.

If we are in a protestant country, we wear the mask of protector of the lutheran religion, and endeavor to make fanatics of the lower order of people, whose simplicity is not proof against our artifice.

In a catholic country, we preach up toleration and moderation, constantly abusing the priests as the cause of all the animosity that exists between the different sectaries, although, in spite of their disputes, they all agree upon material points of faith.

The strength of the parties you may be required to send out, must depend on the confidence that can be placed in the inhabitants of the country. In our country you may run every risk, but more caution and circumspection are necessary in a neutral country, at least till you are convinced of the friendly disposition of the whole, or the greatest part of the peasantry.

In a country that is entirely hostile, as Bohemia and Moravia, you are to hazard nothing, and never send out parties, for the reasons already mentioned, as the people there are not to be trusted any farther than you can see them. The greater part of the light troops are to be employed in guarding the convoys, for you are never to expect to gain the affection of the inhabitants of this country. The Hussites in the circle of Konigingraetz are the only people that can be induced to render us any sort of service. The men of consequence there, though seemingly well disposed towards us, are arrent traitors, nor are the priests or magistrates at all better. As their interest is attached to that of the house of Austria, whose views do not altogether clash with ours, we neither can nor ought to repose any sort of confidence in them.

All that now remains for our management is fanaticism, to know how to inspire a nation with zeal for the liberty of religion, and hint to them in a guarded manner, how much they are oppressed by their great men and priests. This may be said to be moving heaven and hell for one's interest.

Since these notes have been put together, the empress queen has materially increased the taxes in Bohemia and Moravia: advantage may be taken of this circumstance to gain the good-will of the people, especially if we flatter them that they shall be better treated if we become masters of the country.

ARTICLE XV.

Of Every Kind of March, Which It Can Be Necessary for an Army to Make

An army moves for the purposes of advancing in an enemy's country, to take possession of an advantageous camp, join a reinforcement, give battle, or retire before the enemy.

When the camp is properly secured, the next object is to reconnoiter the whole neighborhood and every road that leads from it to camp, that we may be enabled to make the necessary arrangements, as a variety of circumstances may require.

With this view, and under various pretenses, we send out large detachments, accompanied by some engineers and quartermasters, who are to pry into every place that is capable of being occupied by troops. They are also to take up the situation of the country, and reconnoiter the roads by which the troops can march. A certain number of chasseurs should follow them, who are to observe the roads very attentively, that they may be able to lead the columns, provided that the general marches thither.

On their return, the aforesaid officers are to make their report concerning the situation of the camp, the roads that lead to it, the nature of the soil, the woods, mountains, and rivers that are situated thereabouts; and the general, being well informed of all these particulars will make his dispositions accordingly. When the camp is not too near the enemy, the following arrangement may take place.

I suppose that the camp may be approached in four different ways. The advance guard, composed of six battalions of grenadiers, one regiment of infantry, two of dragoons (consisting of five squadrons each), and two regiments of hussars, under the command of Mr. N. N. will depart at eight o'clock this evening. All the encampments of the army are to follow this advance guard, which is to take their tents only with them, leaving their heavy baggage with the army.

These troops are to march four leagues in front and occupy the defile, river, height, town, village, &c. which may be objects of attention,

and wait there the arrival of the army, after
which they are to enter into the camp which has
been already marked out.

On the following morning the army, marching
in four columns, is to move forward after the
advance guard: those men who have been posted
as guards in the villages, falling in with their
respective regiments. The cavalry of the two lines
of the right wing, marching by its right, will form
the first column; the infantry of the two lines of
the right wing, marching by its right, will form
the second; the infantry of the two lines of the left
wing, filing by its right, will form the third; and
the cavalry of the left wing, filing by its right,
will form the fourth column.

The infantry regiments of the second line, and
the three regiments of hussars under the
command of General N. N. will escort the
baggage, which is to march in the rear of the two
columns of infantry.

Four aides-du-camp are to command this
party, who are to take particular care that the
carriages follow each other in order, allowing as
little interval as possible.

If the general commanding the rear guard
should be in want of support, he is immediately
to apply to the commander in chief.

The chasseurs who have reconnoitered the

roads, are to conduct the four columns.

A detachment of carpenters, with wagons laden with beams, joists, and planks, should precede each column, to throw bridges over the small rivers.

The heads of columns must be careful not to go before each other without allowing any intervals. Officers commanding divisions must be attentive in observing their distances.

When you have to pass a defile, the heads of columns must march very slowly, or halt now and then to allow the rear to recover its situation.

It is thus that the order of march is to be conducted.

When mountains, woods, or defiles are met with on the march, the columns are to be divided, and the head, which consists of the infantry, is to be followed by the cavalry, who will close the march.

If there be a plain in the center, it is to be assigned to the cavalry, and the infantry, formed into columns on the two extremities, are to traverse the wood; but this is only to be understood of a march which is made not too near the enemy. In that situation, we are content to place some battalions of grenadiers at the head of each column of cavalry, that they may preserve the order of battle.

The most certain way to insure the safe arrival of a reinforcement is to march through a difficult road to meet it, and to retire from the enemy to avoid an engagement. By means of the superiority which you gain by the arrival of this succour, you will soon recover that ground, which you have, as it were, only lent to the enemy.

When we are obliged to march parallel to the enemy, it must be done in two lines, either by the right or by the left, and each line must form a column, with an advance guard in front. In other respects, those rules which I have just laid down, may also here be employed.

All the marches which we made from Frankenberg to Hohen-Friedberg were directed in this manner, marching to the right.

I prefer these dispositions to any others, because the army can be formed in order of battle by one to the right or one to the left, which is much the readiest way of collecting them, and I would ever practice this method, if I had my choice in attacking the enemy, though I lost the advantage of it at Sohr and at Hohen-Friedberg. In this sort of march, care is to be taken that the flank be never shown to the enemy.

When the enemy begins a march in preparation for an action, you are to disencumber yourself of all your heavy baggage, and send it under escort to the nearest town. The advance guard is then to be formed, and pushed forward to the distance of a short half league.

When the army marches in front against the enemy, care must be taken not only that the columns do not go before each other, but also that when they draw near to the field of battle, they extend themselves in such a manner, that the troops do not take up more or less ground than they will occupy when they are formed. This is a business of much difficulty, as some battalions are generally too much crowded, and others have too much ground allotted them.

Marching by lines is attended with no sort of inconvenience, and on that account has by me ever been preferred.

When we expect to be engaged upon a march, great precaution is required, and it is necessary that the general be very much upon his guard. He should reconnoiter the ground, without exposing himself, from point to point, so as to have an idea of different positions, if the enemy should come to attack him.

Steeples and heights are to be made use of in order to reconnoiter the ground, and the road which leads to them is to be cleared by light troops, detached from the advance guard.

Retreats are generally conducted in the

following manner: A day or two before we depart, the heavy baggage is got together, and sent away under a strong escort.

The number of columns is then to be determined by the number of roads that can be made use of, and the march of the troops regulated by the nature of the ground. In a plain, the advance guard is formed by the cavalry; if it be a chequered country, that post belongs to the infantry. in a plain country, the army will march in four columns.

The infantry of the second line of the right wing, filing by its right, and followed by the second line of the cavalry of the same wing, will form the fourth column. The infantry of the first line of the right wing, filing by its right, will be followed by the first line of cavalry of that wing, and form the third column.

The infantry of the second line of the left wing, followed by the cavalry of that same line, will form the second column. The infantry of the first line of the left wing will be followed by the cavalry of that same line, forming together the first column.

In this manner the rear guard will be formed by the whole of the cavalry, which may be supported, for security's sake by the hussars of the army.

If, during the retreat, it be necessary to pass any defiles, the infantry must occupy them the evening before we depart, and be so posted as to cover the troops, in order that the passage of the defile may remain open.

Supposing that the army marches in two columns, the cavalry of the right will file by its left, the second line moving first, and taking the lead of the second column: the infantry of the second line, followed by the first, will place itself in the rear and follow this cavalry.

The cavalry of the left wing will file by its left, the second line moving first, and heading the first column. This will be joined by the infantry of the left wing, (whose second line will also move before the first,) and thus the first column will be formed.

Six battalions of the rear of the first line, supported by ten squadrons of hussars will form the rear guard. These six battalions are to place themselves in order of battle in front of the defile in two lines.

Whilst the army is passing the defile, the troops that are posted in front must cover and protect by their fire those which still remain on the other side of it.

When the whole army shall have come up, the first line of the advance guard is to throw itself into the defile, having passed through the intervals of the second line; and when it is gone on, the second line will follow in the same manner, under cover of the fire of those who are posted on the other side, who are to follow last, and will form the rear guard.

The most difficult of all maneuvers is that of passing a river during a retreat in presence of the enemy. On this subject I cannot quote a better example than our repassing the Elbe at Kolin in the retreat of 1744.

But as towns are not always in the neighborhood of such situations, I will suppose that your only resource is in two bridges. In such a case a large entrenchment is to be thrown up which will include both bridges, leaving a small opening at the head of each of them.

This being done, we are to send across the river several pieces of cannon with a certain number of troops, and post them on the opposite bank, which should on no account be too steep, but sufficiently elevated to command that which is on the other side. The large entrenchment is then to be lined with infantry, and after such a disposition, the infantry are to be the first to pass over, whilst the cavalry, forming the rear guard, retire in a chequered way through the entrenchment.

When all are passed, the two small heads of the bridge are to be skirted by the infantry, whilst those who are in the entrenchment leave it, in order to retire.

If the enemy have any inclination for a pursuit, he will be exposed to the fire from both heads of the bridge, and from the troops who are posted on the other side of the river.

The infantry who were placed in the entrenchment having passed the river, the bridge is to be destroyed, and the troops who defended the heads of the bridge, are to pass over in boats, under cover of those who are posted on the other side of the river, whose duty it is to advance in order to support them.

When the pontoons are placed on the carriages, the last troops put themselves in motion.

Fougasses [small mines to be fired on leaving entrenchments to render them useless to the enemy] may also be formed at the angles of the entrenchments, which may be set on fire by the last grenadiers at the moment that they have passed the river.

ARTICLE XVI.

On the Precautions Necessary to be Taken in a Retreat Against Hussars and Pandours.

The hussars and pandours [Hungarian foot soldiers] are dreadful only to those who do not know them. They are never brave but when animated by the hope of plunder, or when they can annoy others without exposing themselves. The first species of their bravery they exercise against convoys and baggage, and the other against troops who are obliged to retire, whom they endeavor to tease in their retreat.

Our troops have nothing serious to dread from them, but as a march is often retarded by their manner of skirmishing, and as some men will unavoidably be lost, and that too at a very inconvenient season, I shall explain the best method that I am acquainted with of getting rid of these gentry.

When we retreat through plains, the hussars

are to be driven away by a few discharges of cannon, and the pandours by means of the dragoons and hussars, of whom they are in a very great dread. The most difficult retreats, and those in which the pandours have it in their power to do the greatest mischief, are those where we have to pass woods, defiles, and mountains. In such cases, the loss of some men is almost inevitable.

In these situations, then, the heights should be occupied by the advance guard with their front towards the enemy, and at the same time troops are to be detached on the flank of the line of march, who keeping along on the side of the army will always pass over the heights or through the woods. Some squadrons should also be at hand to be employed where the ground will allow of it.

On these occasions, we are never to halt, but keep constantly moving, for halting would certainly be an unseasonable sacrifice of some of your men.

The pandours fire as they lie down, and by that means keep themselves concealed; and when the marching of the army makes it necessary for the rear guard and the small parties that were detached to quit the heights and follow the main body, they then possess themselves of those situations, and being under cover, pick off those who are retreating. Neither musketry or cannon loaded with cartridge can do them much mischief, as they are scattered and concealed behind the heights and trees.

I made two retreats of this kind in the year 1745; one by the valley of Liebenthal, when marching to Staudenitz, and the other from Trautenau to Schatzlar. Notwithstanding every possible precaution, we lost sixty men killed and wounded in the first retreat, and more than two hundred in the second.

When we have to retreat through difficult ways, our marches should be very short, that we may be the more readily and perfectly on our guard. The longest march should not exceed two leagues, or one German mile, and as then we are not hurried, we are sometimes able to force the pandours, especially if they are imprudent enough to take shelter in a wood, which it is in our power to turn.

ARTICLE XVII.

Of the Method in Which the Light Prussian Troops Conduct Themselves When Engaged with the Hussars and Pandours

Our plan in forcing a post which is occupied by the enemy's light troops is to attack it hastily, for as they disperse in their mode of fighting, they cannot stand against the attack of our regular troops, who are never to mince the matter with them.

We have only to detach a few troops to cover the flanks of the party which marches against them, and then attack them with spirit, to insure their running away.

Our dragoons and hussars attack them closely formed and sword in hand, and as this is a sort of rencontre which they cannot endure, it has always happened that we have beaten them, without paying any regard to the superiority of their numbers.

ARTICLE XVIII.

By What Movements On Our Side the Enemy May Also Be Obliged to Move

We are egregiously mistaken, if we suppose that the mere movement of an army will oblige the enemy also to put himself in motion. This is to be effected not simply by moving, but by the manner in which it is conducted. An intelligent enemy will not be induced to stir on account of any specious maneuvers which you may think proper to practice: Settled positions must be taken up that will oblige him to reflect, and reduce him to the necessity of decamping.

For this reason we should be well informed of the nature of the country, the abilities of the general to whom we are opposed, the situation of his magazines, the towns that are most convenient to him, and those from which he draws his forage; and when these various circumstances are well combined together, the plan is to be formed and maturely digested.

That general who has the most fertile

imagination, and attempts the most frequently to distress his enemy, will eventually rival his antagonist in glory.

He who at the opening of a campaign is the most alert in the assembling of his troops, and marches forward to attack a town or occupy a post, will oblige his adversary to be regulated by his motions, and remain on the defensive.

You must always be possessed of very good reasons for wishing to oblige the enemy to move during a campaign: whether with a view of taking a town near where he is encamped, driving him to a barren country where he will hardly be able to exist, or with the hope of bringing on an engagement which will prove of material advantage. Induced by reasons of this nature, you set about arranging your plan, taking care that the marches which you are to make, and the camps which you are to occupy, do not lead you into greater inconveniencies than the enemy will suffer, by drawing you away from your depot, which may be in a place but badly fortified, and liable to be plundered by the light troops during your absence; by taking up a position where you may be cut off from all communications with your own country, or by occupying a situation which you will soon be obliged to abandon for want of subsistence.

After serious deliberation on these objects, and after having calculated the chances of enterprise on the part of the enemy, your plan is to be arranged, either for the purpose of encamping on one of his flanks, approaching the provinces whence he draws his subsistence, cutting him off from his capital, threatening his depots, or in short, taking up any position by which you deprive him of his provisions.

To give an instance with which the greatest part of my officers are well acquainted, I had formed a plan by which I had reason to hope that I should oblige Prince Charles of Lorraine to abandon Konigingraetz and Pardubitz in the year 1745.

When we quitted the camp at Dubletz, we ought to have gone to the left, passed along by the country of Glatz, and marched near Hohenmauth. By this maneuver we should have forced the Austrians, whose magazines were at Teutschbrod, and whose provisions were, for the most part, drawn from Moravia, to have marched to Landscron, leaving to us Konigingraetz and Pardubitz. The Saxons, being cut off from their home, would have been obliged to quit the Austrians, in order to cover their own country.

What prevented my making this maneuver at that period was, that I should have profited nothing if I had gained Koenigingraetz, as I must have sent detachments to the support of the Prince of Anhalt, in case the Saxons had returned home. Besides this circumstance, the magazines at Glatz were not equal to the subsistence of my army during the whole of the campaign.

The diversions that are made by detaching troops, will also sometimes oblige the enemy to decamp, for generally speaking, every kind of enterprise that comes on him unawares will have the effect of deranging him, and obliging him to quit his position.

Of such nature are the passing of mountains which the enemy deems impassible, and the crossing of rivers without his knowledge.

Sufficient information is to be gained on this head by reading the campaign of Prince Eugene in the year 1701. The confusion of the French army when it was surprised by Prince Charles of Lorraine, who had crossed the Rhine, is a matter sufficiently well understood.

I shall conclude by saying that the execution of enterprises of this nature should always correspond with the design, and as long as the general's dispositions are wise and founded on solid principles, so long will he have it in his power to give the law to his enemy, and oblige him to keep on the defensive.

ARTICLE XIX.

Of the Crossing of Rivers

As long as the enemy remains on the other side of a river which you wish to cross, all force is useless, and recourse must be made to stratagem. To be informed how we are to pass a large river, we have only to consult Caesar's passage of the Rhine, that of the Po by Prince Eugene, or of the Rhine by Prince Charles of Lorraine. These generals sent out detachments to impose upon the enemy, and conceal the spot where they intended to pass. They made every preparation for the building of bridges in places where they had no idea of employing them, whilst the main body of the army, by a night march, gained a considerable distance from the enemy, and had time to pass the river before the troop, who were to dispute their passage, could be put in order to prevent them.

We generally choose to cross rivers at those parts where there are some small islands, as they forward the business very materially. We wish also to meet on the other side with woods or other obstacles, that may prevent the enemy from attacking us before we have had time to get into proper order.

The most prudent measures and the most particular attention are required in enterprises of this nature. The boats or pontoons with every other article of necessary apparatus must be at the rendezvous by the appointed hour, and every boatman well instructed what generally attends expeditions by night. Everything being arranged, the troops are to pass over and establish themselves on the other side of the river.

Whenever rivers are to be crossed, care should be taken that the two heads of the bridge be entrenched, and well furnished with troops. The islands which are in the neighborhood should be fortified, in order to support the entrenchments, and prevent the enemy, during your operations, from seizing or destroying the bridges.

If the rivers be narrow, we choose our passage at those parts where they form angles, and where the bank, by being a little more elevated, commands that on the opposite side.

On this spot we place as many cannon, with a proportionate number of troops, as the ground will allow, under the protection of which the bridges are to be built; and as the ground grows narrower on account of the angle, we are to advance but very little, and insensibly gain ground as the troops pass.

If there be any fords, we slope the ground leading to them, to enable the cavalry to pass.

ARTICLE XX.

Of the Manner in Which the Passage of Rivers is to Be Defended

Nothing is more difficult, not to say impossible, than to defend the passage of a river, especially when the front of attack be of too great an extent. I would never undertake a commission of this kind, if the ground which I had to defend was more than eight German miles in front, and unless there were two or three redoubts established on the bank of the river within this distance; neither should any other part of the river be fordable.

But supposing the situation to be exactly as I have stated, time must always be required to make the necessary preparations against the enterprises of the enemy, the disposition of which should be nearly as follows.

All the boats and barks which can be found upon the river should be got together and conveyed to the two redoubts, that the enemy may not have it in his power to make use of them.

Both banks of the river are to be reconnoitered, that you may discover and destroy those parts of them where it would be possible to pass.

The ground which might protect the passage of the enemy is to be particularly attended to, and your plans of attack must be regulated by the nature and situation of each part of it.

Roads sufficiently wide to admit of many columns are to be made along the whole front of the river which you are to defend, that you may march against the enemy free of every impediment.

These precautions being taken, the army is to be encamped in the center of the line of defense, that you may have but four miles to march to either extremity. Sixteen small detachments are then to be formed, and commanded by the most active, intelligent officers of dragoons and hussars; eight of which, under the orders of a general officer, are to have charge of the front of attack on the right, whilst the other eight, commanded in like manner, take care of the left.

These detachments will be designed to give information of the enemy's movements, and of the spot where it will be his intention to pass.

During the day, guards are to be posted to discover what is going forward, and by night patrols are to go out every quarter of an hour near to the river, and not retire till they have distinctly seen that the enemy has made a bridge, and that the head has passed.

The aforesaid generals and commanding officers of redoubts are to send their reports to the commander in chief four times a day.

Fresh horses should be stationed between them and the army, in order to hasten the arrival of their dispatches, and inform the general as immediately as possible when the enemy is about to pass. As it is the duty of the general to repair thither at a moment's warning, his baggage should be sent away beforehand, that he may be ready for every event.

The different dispositions for each part of the ground being already made, the generals are appointed by the commander in chief to those which regard the points of attack. No time is to be lost in marching, (the infantry taking the lead of the columns), as you are to suppose that the enemy are entrenching themselves. When arrived, the attack is to be made instantly and with great spirit, as the only means of promising to yourself brilliant success.

The passages of small rivers are still more difficult to defend; their fords are to be rendered impassible, if possible, by throwing in of trees.

But if the enemy's bank commands yours it is vain to attempt resistance.

ARTICLE XXI.

Of the Surprise of Towns

A town must be badly guarded and weakly fortified that suffers a surprise; and if its ditches be filled with water, the success of such enterprises must depend on a wintry season and hard frost.

Towns may be surprised by a whole army, as was the case at Prague in the year 1741, or the accident may happen from the garrison having been lulled into security by a long continued blockade, as was effected by Prince Leopold d'Anhalt at Glogau. Detachments also sometimes have the desired effect, as was attempted by Prince Eugene at Cremona, and as succeeded with the Austrians at Cosel.

The principal rule in making dispositions for surprise is to be well informed of the nature of the fortifications and of the interiors of the place, so as to direct your attack to any particular spot.

The surprise of Glogau was a chef d'oeuvre, and is well worth the imitation of those who attempt such enterprises. There was nothing so extraordinary in the surprise of Prague, as it was impossible that such a variety of attacks must carry a place, where the garrison had so great an extent to defend. Cosel and Cremona were betrayed; the first by an officer who deserted and informed the Austrians that the excavation of the ditch was not quite completed, by which means they got over, and the place was carried.

If we wish to take small places, we batter some of the gates with mortars, whilst detachments are sent to the others to prevent the garrison from saving themselves.

If cannon are to be employed, they must be so placed that the artillerymen be not exposed to the fire of the musketry; otherwise the guns will be in danger of being lost.

ARTICLE XXII.

Of Combats and Battles

The Austrian camp is surrounded by such a number of light troops, as to render a surprise a work of very great difficulty.

If two armies keep near to each other, the business will very soon be decided, unless one of them occupies an inaccessible post that will secure it from surprises; a circumstance which seldom takes place between armies, though it be nothing uncommon between detachments.

To have it in our power to surprise an enemy in his camp, it is necessary that he relies entirely either on the superiority of his troops, the advantageous situation of his post, the reports of his emissaries, or lastly, on the vigilance of his light troops.

The nature of the country and the position of the enemy should be perfectly well understood prior to the formation of any plan.

The roads leading to camp must be well examined, and the general disposition of things formed from thence, being regulated in every point by the particular and exact knowledge of all attendant circumstances.

The most intelligent chasseurs, who are best acquainted with the roads, should be appointed to conduct the columns.

Be particularly careful to conceal your design, for secrecy is the soul of all enterprises.

The light troops should take the lead on the march, for which regulation various reasons may be assigned, though the real one be to prevent any scoundrel of a deserter from betraying you. They will also be of service by preventing the enemy's patrols from approaching too nearly and discovering your movements.

The generals who are under your orders must be well instructed of all events that may happen, and how to act when any accident occurs.

If the enemy's camp be situated in a plain, an advance guard may be formed of dragoons, who, being joined by the hussars, will enter the enemy's camp on full speed, throw it into confusion, and cut down whatever comes in their way.

The whole army should support these dragoons, and the infantry being at the head of it, should be particularly employed in attacking the wings of the enemy's cavalry.

The advance guard should begin the attack half an hour before day, but the army should not be more than eight hundred yards in its rear.

During the march the most profound silence is to be observed, and the soldiers must be forbidden to smoke tobacco.

When the attack has commenced and the day appears, the infantry, formed into four or six columns, must march straight forward to the camp, in order to support its advance guard.

No firing is to be allowed before daylight, as it might prove the means of destroying our own people: but as soon as the day is broke, we should fire on all those places into which the advance guard has not penetrated, especially on the wings of the cavalry, that we may oblige the troopers, who have not time to accoutre their horses, to abandon them and fly.

The enemy are to be followed even out of their camp, and the whole of the cavalry should be let loose after them to take advantage of their disorder and confusion.

If the enemy have abandoned their arms, a strong detachment must be left in charge of the camp, whilst the remainder of the army, instead of amusing themselves with plunder, pursue the enemy with all possible ardor; the more so, as a like opportunity of entirely routing them, may not soon present itself, and we may, by so doing, have the upper hand during the whole campaign, and be able to act just as we think proper.

Fortune intended to favor me with an opportunity of this kind before the battle of Mollwitz: we approached the army of the Marshal de Neuperg without being perceived, as they were cantoned in three villages; but at that time I wanted information how to profit by such circumstance.

My business then was, to have surrounded the village of Mollwitz by two columns, and to have attacked it. At the same moment I should have detached some dragoons to the other two villages where the Austrian cavalry lay, in order to throw them into confusion, whilst the infantry who followed them would have prevented the cavalry from mounting. By this method I am persuaded the whole army would have been destroyed.

I have already shown the necessary cautions that respect our camp, and the manner in which it is to be protected: but if in spite of all our care, the enemy should approach the army, I would advise that the troops be formed in order of battle on the ground which is allotted to them, and that the cavalry remain firm on their posts, firing by platoons till daybreak. The generals are then to examine whether it be advisable to advance, if the cavalry has been victorious or suffered a repulse, and what further methods are to be pursued.

On such occasions, each general should know how to act independently, without being obliged to wait for the instructions of the commander-in-chief.

For my own part, I am determined never to attack by night, on account of the confusion which darkness necessarily occasions, and because the major part of the soldiery require the eye of their officers, and the fear of punishments, to induce them to do their duty.

Charles XII in the year 1715, attacked the Prince of Anhalt in the night, though he was but just disembarked on the island of Rugen. The King of Sweden had reason for so doing, as day-light would have discovered the weakness of his army. He came with four thousand men to attack five times the number, and of course was defeated.

It is an invariable axiom of war, to secure your flanks and rear, and endeavor to turn those of your enemy. This may be done in different ways, though they all depend on the same principle.

When you are obliged to attack an entrenched enemy, it should be done instantly, without allowing him time to finish his works. What would be of advantage today, may not be so tomorrow.

But before you set about making the attack,

the enemy's position must be well reconnoitered
with your own eyes, and your first dispositions
of attack will convince you whether your scheme
will be easily put into execution, or become a
work of labor and difficulty.

The want of sufficient support is the chief
reason that entrenchments are taken. The
entrenchment of Turenne was carried, as was also
that of [Schellenberg] because there was sufficient
ground to enable the Prince of Anhalt to turn it.
That of Malplaquet was turned by the wood
which was on Marshal Villers' left. Had the allies
been aware of this circumstance at the beginning
of the battle, it would have saved their army
fifteen thousand men.

If a fordable river support the entrenchment,
it must be attacked on that side. The work at
Stralsund, conducted by the Swedes, was carried
because the attack was made on the sea-side,
where it happened to be fordable.

If the enemy's entrenchments are of too great
an extent, so that the troops are obliged to
occupy more ground than they can well defend,
we attack at several points, and provided we
can keep our designs secret from the enemy
(which will prevent his meeting us with a
sufficient force), we shall certainly get
possession of the works.

I shall form the line with thirty battalions, and strengthen the left wing by the river. The attack on the left, where I wish to penetrate, shall be made by twelve battalions, and that on the right by eight. The troops destined for the attack are to be formed in a chequered way, with the allowance of proper intervals. The remainder of the infantry are to throw themselves into the third line, and behind them, at the distance of four hundred yards, the cavalry should be posted. By this means my infantry will keep the enemy in check, and be ready to take advantage of any false movement which he may make.

Care must be taken that each of these attacks be followed closely by a number of pioneers with shovels, pickaxes, and fascines to fill up the ditch, and make a road for the cavalry, when the entrenchment shall have been forced.

The infantry who form the attack are not to fire till the work is carried, and they are drawn up in order of battle on the parapet.

The cavalry are to enter through the openings made by the pioneers, and attack the enemy as soon as they find themselves of sufficient force. If the cavalry be repulsed, they must rally under the cover of the infantry's fire until the whole army has got in, and the enemy are entirely routed.

I must here repeat, that I would never entrench my army unless I had a siege in contemplation; and I am not decided, whether it be not the best plan to go on before the army that comes to relieve a place.

But supposing for a moment, that we have an inclination to entrench ourselves; to execute such intention, the following method appears to me the most advantageous.

We contrive to have two or three large reserves, which are to be sent out during the attack to those points where the enemy is making his greatest efforts.

The parapet is to be lined by battalions, and a reserve placed behind them, to be at hand in case of necessity. The cavalry should be ranged in one line behind these reserves.

The entrenchments should be very well supported, and if it be joined by a river, the ditch should be carried some distance into it, to prevent its being turned.

If it be strengthened by a wood, it should be closed at that end by a redoubt, and a large abbatis of trees should also be made in the wood.

Particular regard must be paid to the flanking of the redans.

The ditch should be very deep and wide, and the entrenchments must be improved every day, either by strengthening the parapet, placing palisades at the entrance of the barriers, digging of pits, or furnishing the whole of the camp with chevaux-de-frize.

The greatest advantage you have is in the choice of your work and in the observance of certain rules of fortification which will oblige the enemy to attack you on a small front, and that only in the principal points of your entrenchment.

The army, which is there placed at the head of the entrenchment, is thrown back on one side by the river, so that you present a projecting front to the enemy who comes to attack you. Your right is safe from attack by means of the batteries placed at the extremities of that wing, which would play upon the enemy's flank, whilst the center redoubt would take him in the rear. The only point liable to attack therefore is the center redoubt, and even here he will be obliged to cut his way through the abbatis.

In your preparations for this attack it behooves you therefore to strengthen the fortifications of this redoubt, and as you have but one point which demands your particular attention, that one will consequently be more perfect and complete.

Entrenchments of a different kind are

composed of projecting and receding redoubts, which cross each other, and are connected by entrenchments.

By this method of fortification, those that project from the point of attack, and as they are but few of them, much less time is required in completing them, than if the whole front was to be equally well fortified.

In these projecting redoubts, the fire of the musketry must always cross each other, and for this reason they should never be more than six hundred yards apart.

Our infantry defend an entrenchment by the fire of entire battalions, and every soldier should be provided with one hundred rounds. This, however, is not to prevent placing as many cannon as we can between the battalions and the projecting redoubts.

Whilst the enemy are at a distance, we fire shot, but when they approach within four hundred yards, we have recourse to cartridges.

If, notwithstanding the strength of your entrenchment, and the smartness of your fire, the enemy should make any impression, the reserve of infantry must march forward to repel him, and if they also be obliged to fall back, your last effort to put him to the route must depend upon your cavalry.

The principal reasons why entrenchments are carried are these, the want of attention to proper rules in their construction, or the troops being turned or panic struck: the superior freedom and boldness with which the attackers are able to conduct themselves, gives them this advantage.

Examples have already shown, that when an entrenchment is forced, the whole army is discouraged and put to flight: I have a better opinion of my troops, and am persuaded that they would repel the enemy; but what end would this answer, if the entrenchments prevent their profiting by such advantages?

As there are so many inconveniencies attending entrenchments, it naturally follows that lines are still more useless. The fashion of our day is that which was practiced by Prince Louis de Baden, whose first lines were made on the side of Briel. The French also employed them after that in Flanders. I maintain that they are of no service whatever, since they compass more ground than the troops can possibly defend; they allow of a variety of attacks being made on them, and tempt the enemy to force a passage. On this account they do not cover the country, but, on the contrary, ensure the loss of reputation to the troops who have to defend them.

Although a Prussian army should be inferior

to that which is opposed to them, they are not to despair of success, as the general's management will supply the want of numbers.

An army that is weak should always make choice of a difficult, mountainous country, where the ground narrows, so that the superior number of the enemy, not being able to pass their wings, becomes useless, and often an incumbrance to them.

It may here be added, that in a country which is close and hilly, the wings can better be supported than when we are on a plain. We should not have gained the battle of Sohr but for the advantage of the ground, for though the Austrian army doubled ours, they were not able to break through our wings, as the ground rendered both the armies nearly equal.

The choice of ground is my first object, and my second the disposition of the battle itself; it is here that my oblique order of battle may be employed to advantage, for you to refuse one wing to the enemy, whilst you strengthen that which ought to make the attack. By this means you turn all your force on that wing of the enemy which you wish to take in flank.

An army of ten thousand men, if its flanks are turned, will very soon be defeated. Every thing is done by my right wing. A body of infantry will move by degrees into the wood, to attack the flanks of the enemy's cavalry, and protect the onset of our own: some regiments of hussars should be ordered to take the enemy in the rear whilst the army advances, and when their cavalry are routed, the infantry who are in the wood must take the enemy's infantry in flank, whilst the remainder are attacking them in front.

My left wing will not stir till the enemy's left wing is entirely defeated.

By this disposition you will gain the following advantages: 1st, that of making head with a small force against a much superior number; 2dly, of attacking the enemy at a point which will decide the business; 3dly, if your wing should chance to be beaten, as only a small part of your army has been engaged, three-fourths of your troops, who are fresh, will be ready to support you in your retreat.

If you wish to attack an enemy that is advantageously posted, you must carefully examine both his strong and weak side before you make your dispositions for attack, and always choose that point where you expect to meet with the least resistance.

So many men are lost in the attacks on villages, that I have vowed never to undertake them, unless obliged by absolute necessity, for you run the hazard of losing the flower of your infantry.

It is said by some generals, that the most proper point of attack is the center of a post, where I suppose the enemy to have two large towns and two villages on its wings. The wings must certainly be lost, when you have forced the center, and by similar attacks, the most complete victories may be obtained.

If must be added to the plan which I here lay down, that you must double your attack when you have once made an impression, in order to force the enemy to fall back both on his right and upon his left.

Nothing is so formidable in the attack of a post, as the discharge of cartridges from the batteries, which made a terrible havoc amongst the battalions. I witnessed the attacks on the batteries of Sohr and Kesseldorf, and shall here communicate the idea suggested by my reflections on that business, supposing that we wish to be possessed of a battery mounted with fifteen pieces of cannon, which it is not in our power to turn.

I have remarked that the fire of cannon and of infantry who defend a battery render it inaccessible. We cannot make ourselves masters of the enemy's batteries but through their own fault: finding our infantry who attacked half destroyed and giving way, the infantry of the enemy quit their post to follow them, and being by this movement deprived of the use of their cannon, when they return to their batteries, our people enter with them and take possession.

The experience of those two battles gave me the idea that in similar cases we should copy the example of our troops on this occasion, to form the attack in two lines in a chequered way, and to be supported in the third line by some squadrons of dragoons.

The first line should be ordered to attack but faintly, and fall back through the intervals of the second, so that the enemy, deceived by this sham retreat, may abandon his post in order to pursue us.

This movement of theirs is to be our signal to advance and make a vigorous attack.

It is my principle, never to place my whole confidence in one post, unless it can be physically proved to be safe from any attack.

The great dependence of our troops is in attacking, and we should act very foolish to give up this point without good reason.

But if it be necessary that posts should be occupied, we remember to get possession of the heights, and make our wings sufficiently strong.

I would burn every village which is at the head or on the wings of the army, if the wind did not drive the smoke into the camp.

If there were any strong stone houses in front, I would defend them by the infantry, in order to annoy the enemy during the action.

Great care should be taken, not to place troops on ground where they cannot act; it was this which made our position at Grotkau in the year 1741 worth nothing, for the center and left wing were posted behind impassible bogs. The only ground that would admit of being maneuverd on, was that which was occupied by a part of the right wing.

Villeroy was beaten at Ramillies for the very reason that I have just mentioned, as his right wing was rendered entirely useless, and the enemy crowded all its force against the right wing of the French which could make no resistance.

I allow the Prussian troops to take possession of advantageous posts as well as other troops, and to make use of them in favor of any movement, or to take advantage of their artillery; but they must quit this post instantly to march against the enemy, who instead of being allowed to begin the attack, is attacked himself, and sees all his projects miscarry. Every movement which we make in presence of the enemy without his expecting it, will certainly produce a good effect.

We must rank battles of this kind amongst the best, always remembering to attack the weakest point.

On these occasions, I would not permit the infantry to fire, for it only retards their march, and the victory is not decided by the number of slain, but by the extent of territory which you have gained.

The most certain way of insuring victory is to march briskly and in good order against the enemy, always endeavoring to gain ground. It is the custom to allow fifteen yards of interval between squadrons in a difficult, intersected country, but where the ground is good and even, they form in a line entire.

No greater interval is to be allowed between the infantry than is sufficient for the cannon. It is only in attacks of entrenchment, batteries, and villages, and in the formation of the rear guard in a retreat, that the cavalry and infantry are placed in a chequered way, in order to give an immediate support to the first line by making the second fall into its intervals, so that the troops may retire without disorder, and be a mutual support to each other. This is a rule never to be neglected.

An opportunity offers itself here of giving you some principal rules on what you are to observe when you range the army in order of battle, whatever the ground may happen to be. The first is to take up points of view for the wings; the right wing, for example, will align itself by the steeple.

The general must be particularly careful that he does not suffer the troops to take up a wrong position.

It is not always necessary to defer the attack till the whole army can engage, as opportunity may present advantages which would be lost by a little delay.

A great part of the army, however, ought to be engaged, and the first line should be the chief object in the regulation of the order of battle. If all the regiments of that line are not present, they should be replaced by the same number of the second.

The wings should always be well supported, especially those which are expected to make the greatest exertions.

In an open country, the order of battle should be equally strong throughout, for as the enemy's movements are unconfined, he may have reserved a part of his army which he may make use of to cut you out a little employment.

In case that one of the two wings should not be properly supported, the general who commands the second line should send some dragoons thither (without waiting for an order on the occasion) to extend the first line, and the hussars taken from the third line should replace the dragoons.

The reason for so doing is that if the enemy make a movement to take the cavalry of the first line in flank, your dragoons and hussars may be able in turn to repay the compliment.

I place three battalions in the interval between the two lines of the left wing, the better to support it: for supposing your cavalry to be beaten, these battalions will always prevent the enemy from falling foul on the infantry, an instance of which we witnessed at Mollwitz.

The general commanding the second line must preserve a distance of three hundred paces from the first, and if he perceive any intervals in the first line, he is to fill them up with battalions from the second.

In a plain, a reserve of cavalry should always be placed in the rear of the center of the battalions, and be commanded by an officer of address, as he is to act from himself, either in support of a wing that he sees hardly pressed, or by flanking the enemy who are in pursuit of the wing that is thrown into disorder, that the cavalry may in the meantime have an opportunity of rallying.

The affair should be begun by the cavalry on full gallop, and the infantry also should march on briskly towards the enemy. Commanding officers are to take care that their troops penetrate and entirely break through the enemy, and that they make no use of their firearms till their backs are turned.

If the soldiers fire without the word of command, they are to be ordered to shoulder arms, and proceed without any halting.

When the enemy begins to give way, we fire, by battalions, and a battle conducted in this manner will very soon be decided.

A new order of battle ensues, which differs from the others in having bodies of infantry placed at the extremities of the wings of the cavalry. The battalions are intended to support the cavalry, by playing with their own cannon and those belonging to the wings of the cavalry, on the enemy's cavalry, at the beginning of the affair, that our own may have a better game to play during the attack. Another reason is that supposing your wings to be beaten, the enemy dare not pursue, for fear of being between two fires.

When your cavalry, to all appearance, has

been victorious, this infantry is to approach that of the enemy, and the battalions which are in the intervals must make a quarter-wheel and place themselves on your wings, to take the enemy's infantry in flank and rear, and enable you to make a handsome business of it.

The conquering wing of your cavalry must not allow the enemy's cavalry to rally, but pursue them in good order, and endeavor to cut them off from the infantry. When the confusion becomes general, the commanding officer should detach the hussars after them, who are to be supported by the cavalry. At the same time some dragoons should be sent to the roads which the infantry have taken, in order to pick them up, and by cutting off their retreat, make a great number of them prisoners.

There is another difference in this order of battle, which is, that the squadrons of dragoons are mixed with the infantry of the second line: this is done, because I have remarked in all the affairs which we have had with the Austrians, that after the fire of their musketry has continued for about a quarter of an hour, they get together round their colors; at Hohen-Friedburg our cavalry charged many of these round-about parties, and made a great number of them prisoners. The dragoons, being near at hand, are to be let loose instantly, and they never fail to give a very good account of themselves.

It will be said, that I never employ my small arms, but that it is my wish in all these dispositions to make use of my artillery only: to this I answer, that one of the two accidents which I suppose will unavoidably happen, either that my infantry fire in spite of my orders to the contrary, or that they obey my commands, and the enemy begins to give way. In either case, as soon as you perceive any confusion amongst their troops, you are to detach the cavalry after them, and when they find themselves attacked in flank on one side, charged in front, and their second line of cavalry cut off by the rear, the greatest part of them will be sure to fall into your hands.

It then cannot be called a battle, but an entire destruction of your enemies, especially if there be no defile in the neighborhood to protect their flight.

I shall close this article with a single reflection, viz. if you march to battle in column, whether by the right or by the left, the battalions or divisions must follow each other closely, that when you begin to deploy, you may have it in your power readily to engage. But if you march in front, the distances of the battalions must be well attended to, that they be not too close or too far from each other.

I make a distinction between the heavy cannon and the field pieces attached to the battalions, as the former should be planted on the heights, and the latter fifty paces in front of the battalions. Both the one and the other should be well pointed and well fired.

When we are within five hundred yards of the enemy, the field pieces should be drawn by men, that they may fire without intermission as we advance.

If the enemy begin to fly, the heavy cannon are to move forward and fire a few rounds, by way of wishing them a good journey.

Six gunners and three regimental carpenters should be attached to every piece in the first line.

I had omitted saying, that at the distance of three hundred and fifty yards, the cannon should begin to fire cartridges.

But to what end serves the art of conquest, if we are ignorant how to profit by our advantage? To shed the blood of soldiers when there is no occasion for it, is to lead them inhumanly to the slaughter; and not to pursue the enemy on certain occasions, to increase their fear and the number of our prisoners, is leaving an affair to future chance which might be determined at the present moment. Nevertheless, you may sometimes be prevented from pursuing your conquest by a want of provisions, or the troops being too much fatigued.

It is always the fault of the general-in-chief if an army want provisions. When he gives battle, he has a design in so doing: and if he has a design, it is his duty to be provided with every thing necessary for the execution of it, and of course he ought to be supplied with bread or biscuit for eight or ten days.

With respect to fatigue, if they had not been too excessive, they must not be regarded, as on extraordinary occasions extraordinary feats should be performed.

When victory is perfectly decided, I would recommend a detachment to be made of those regiments who have been the greatest sufferers, to take care of the wounded, and convey them to the hospitals, which ought to be already established. Though our own wounded are to be the first objects of our attention, we are not to forget our duty to the enemy.

In the meantime the army is to pursue the enemy to the nearest defile, which in the first transport of their alarm they will not tarry to keep possession of, if you take care not to allow them sufficient time to recover their wind.

When you have attended to all these circumstances, the camp is to be marked out, paying strict regard to the established rules, and not allowing yourself to be lulled with too great an idea of security.

If the victory has been complete, we may send out detachments either to cut off the enemy's retreat, seize his magazines, or lay siege to three or four towns at the same time.

On this article, general rules only can be given, as a great deal must depend on fortuitous circumstances. You are never to imagine that everything is done as long as anything remains undone; nor are you to suppose but that a cunning enemy, though he may have been beaten, will keep a sharp lookout to take advantage of your negligence or errors.

I pray to heaven, that the Prussians never may be beaten, and dare affirm that such an accident never will happen if they are well led on and well disciplined.

But should they meet with a disaster of such a nature, the following rules are to be observed in order to recover the misfortune. When you see that the battle is inevitably lost, and that it is not in your power to oppose the enemy's movements, or even resist them much longer, you are to send the second line of infantry to any defile that may be near, and place them in it agreeably to the disposition which I have given under the article of retreats, sending thither at the same time as many cannon as you can spare.

If there be no defile in the neighborhood, the first line must retire through the interval of the second, and place itself in order of battle three hundred yards behind them.

All the remains of your cavalry must be got together, and if you choose it, they may be formed into a square to protect your retreat.

History furnishes us with accounts of two remarkable squares: one that was formed by General Schullembourg after the battle of Frauenstadt, by means of which he retired across the Oder without being forced by Charles XII; the other by the Prince of Anhalt when General Stirum lost the first battle of Hochstaedt. This Prince traversed a plain of two leagues, and the French cavalry did not dare to molest him.

I shall conclude with saying, that though we are defeated, there is no occasion for running away forty leagues, but that we are to halt at the first advantageous post, and put a bold face upon the business, in order to collect the scattered army, and encourage those who are dispirited.

ARTICLE XXIII.

Of the Reasons Which Should Induce Us to Give Battle and in What Manner It Is to Be Conducted

Battles determine the fate of nations. It is necessary that actions should be decisive, either to free ourselves from the inconveniencies of a state of warfare, to place our enemy in that unpleasant situation, or to settle a quarrel which otherwise perhaps would never be finished. A man that is wise will make no sort of movement without good reason; and a general of an army should never be engaged without some design of consequence. If he be forced into an engagement by his adversary, his former errors must have reduced him to that situation, and given his enemy the power of dictating the law to him.

On the present occasion it will be seen, that I am not writing my own panegyric: for out of five battles which my troops have given to the enemy, three of them only were premeditated, and I was forced by the enemy into the other two. At the affair of Mollwitz the Austrians had posted themselves between my army and Wohlau, where I kept my provisions and artillery. At that of the Sohr, the enemy had cut me off from the road to Trautenau, so that I was obliged to fight, or run the risk of losing my whole army. But how great is the difference between forced and premeditated battles! How brilliant was our success at Hohen-Friedberg, at Kesseldorf, and also at Czaslau, which last engagement was the means of procuring us peace!

Though I am here laying down rules for battles, I do not pretend to deny that I have often erred through inadvertence; my officers, however, are expected to profit by my mistakes, and they may be assured, that I shall apply myself with all diligence to correct them.

It sometimes happens that both the armies wish to engage, and then the business is very soon settled.

Those battles are the best into which we force the enemy, for it is an established maxim, to oblige him to do that for which he has no sort of inclination, and as your interest and his are so diametrically opposite, it cannot be supposed that you are both wishing for the same event.

Many are the reasons that may induce us to give battle, such as, a desire to oblige the enemy to raise the siege of any place that may prove of convenience to yourself, to drive him out of a province which he possesses, penetrate his country, enable yourself to lay a siege, correct him for his stubbornness if he refuse to make peace, or make him suffer for some error that he has committed.

You will also oblige the enemy to come to action when, by a forced march, you fall upon his rear and cut off his communications, or by threatening a town which it is his interest to preserve.

But in this sort of maneuver great care is to be taken that you do not get into the same embarrassed situation, or take up a position which enables the enemy to cut you off from your magazines.

The affairs which are undertaken against rear guards are attended with the least danger.

If you entertain a design of this nature, you are to encamp near the enemy, and when he wishes to retire and pass the defiles in your presence, make an attack upon his rear. Much advantage is often gained by engagements of this kind.

It is also a custom to tease and tire the enemy,

in order to prevent different bodies from forming a junction. The object in view sufficiently warrants such attempt, but a skillful enemy will have the address to get out of your way by a forced march, or escape the accident by taking up an advantageous position.

Sometimes when you have no inclination to fight, we are induced to it by the misconduct of the enemy, who should always be punished for his faults, if we can profit by so doing.

It must be urged, in addition to all these maxims, that our wars should ever be of short duration, and conducted with spirit, for it must always be against our interest to be engaged in a tedious affair. A long war must tend insensibly to relax our admirable discipline, depopulate our country, and exhaust its resources.

For this reason, generals commanding Prussian armies should endeavor, notwithstanding their success, to terminate every business prudently and quickly. They must not argue, as the Marshal de Luxembourg did in the Flanders wars, who when he was told by his son, "Father, it appears to me, that we could still take another town," replied, "Hold your tongue, you little fool! Would you have us go home to plant cabbages?" In a word, on the subject of battles, we ought to be guided by the maxim of Sannerib of the Hebrews, "that it is better one man perish than a whole people."

With regard to punishing an enemy for his fault, we should consult the relation of the battle of Senef, where the Prince of Conde brought on an affair of the rear guard against the Prince of Orange or the Prince of Waldeck, who had neglected to occupy the head of a defile, in order to facilitate his retreat.

The accounts of the battle of ..., gained by the Marshal de Luxembourg, and that of Raucoux, will also furnish you with other examples.

ARTICLE XXIV.

Of the Hazards and Unforeseen Accidents Which Happen in War

This article would be of a melancholy length, if it was my intention to treat of all the accidents which might happen to a general in war. I shall cut the matter short by saying, that it is necessary a man should have both address and good fortune.

Generals are much more to be pitied than is generally imagined. All the world condemns them unheard. They are exposed in the gazette to the judgment of the meanest plebeian, whilst amongst many thousand readers there is not one perhaps who knows how to conduct the smallest detachment.

I shall not pretend to excuse those generals who have been in fault; I shall even give up my own campaign of 1744, but I must add, that though I have many times erred, I have made some good expeditions; for example, the siege of Prague, the defense and the retreat of Koelin, and again the retreat in Silesia. I shall not enter further into these actions, but must observe, that there are accidents which neither the most mature reflection or keenest human foresight can possibly prevent.

As I write at present solely for my own generals, I shall not quote other examples than what have occurred to myself. When we were at Reichenbach, I intended to have reached the river Neiss by a forced march, and to have posted myself between the town of that name and the army of General de Neuperg, in order to cut off his communication. All the necessary dispositions were arranged for such operation, but a heavy fall of rain came on which made the roads so very bad, that our advance guard with the pontoons were unable to proceed. During the march of the army also so thick a fog arose, that the troops who were posted as guards in the villages wandered about without being able to join their respective regiments. In short, every thing turned out so ill, that instead of arriving at four o'clock A.M. as I had intended, we did not get there till midnight. The advantages to be derived from a forced march were then out of the question, the enemy had the start of us, and defeated our project.

If, during your operations, disease should

break out amongst your troops, you will be obliged to act on the defensive, which was the case with us in Bohemia in the year 1741, on account of the badness of the provisions with which the troops were furnished.

At the battle of Hohen-Friedberg, I ordered one of my aides-de-camp [flugel-adjutants] to go to Margrave Charles, and tell him to place himself, as eldest general, at the head of my second line, because General Kalckstein had been detached to the command of the right wing against the Saxons: this aide-de-camp mistook the business entirely, and ordered the margrave to form the first line into the second. By great good fortune I discovered the mistake, and had time to remedy it.

Hence we see the necessity of being always on our guard, and of bearing in mind that a commission badly executed may disconcert all our intentions.

If a general fall sick, or be killed, at the head of a detachment of any importance, many of your measures must consequently suffer a very material derangement. To act offensively requires generals of sound understanding and genuine valor, the number of which is but very small: I have at the most but three or four such in my whole army.

If, in spite of every precaution, the enemy should succeed in depriving you of some convoy, your plans will again be disconcerted, and your project either suspended or entirely overset.

Should circumstances oblige the army to fall back, the troops will be very much discouraged.

I have never been so unhappy as to experience a situation of this sort with my whole army, but I remarked at the battle of Mollwitz, that it required a length of time to reanimate troops who had been disheartened. At that time my cavalry was so weakened, that they looked on themselves as merely led to the slaughter, which induced me to send out small detachments to give them spirits, and bring them forward to action. It is only since the battle of Hohen-Friedberg, that my cavalry are become what they ever ought to be, and what they are at present.

If the enemy should discover a spy of any consequence in their camp, the compass is lost which was to have directed you, and you are unable to learn anything of the enemy's movements but from your own eyes.

The negligence of officers who are detached to reconnoiter may render your situation very distressed and embarrassing. It was in this way that Marshal de Neuperg was surprised; the hussar officer who was sent forward on the lookout had neglected his duty, and we were close upon him before he had the least suspicion of it. It was also owing to the carelessness of an officer of the regiment of Ziethen in making his patrol by night, that the enemy built his bridges at Selmitz, and surprised the baggage.

Hence will appear the truth of my assertion that the safety of a whole army should never be entrusted to the vigilance of an individual officer. No one man or subaltern officer should be charged with a commission of such material consequence. Treasure up, therefore, carefully in your mind what I have said on this subject under the article, "Of the Defense of Rivers."

Too much confidence must not be reposed in patrols and reconnoitering parties, but in measures of more surety and solidity.

The greatest possible misfortune that can attend an army is treason. Prince Eugene was betrayed in the year 1733 by General St. ... who had been corrupted by the French. I lost Cosel through the treachery of an officer of the garrison who deserted and conducted the enemy thither. Hence we are taught, that even in the height of our prosperity, it is not safe to trust to good fortune, or wise to be too much elevated with success; we should rather recollect, that the slender portion of genius and foresight which we may possess is at best but a game of hazard and unforeseen accidents, by which it pleases, I know not what destiny, to humble the pride of presumptuous man.

ARTICLE XXV.

If It Be Absolutely Necessary That the General of an Army Should Hold a Council of War

It was a saying of Prince Eugene, "that if a general did not wish to fight, he had nothing more to do than hold a council of war;" and his assertion is proved, by the general voice of councils of war being against engaging. Secrecy, so necessary in war, can here be no longer observed.

A general, to whom his sovereign has entrusted his troops, should act for himself, and the confidence placed in him by his king is a sufficient warrant for such conduct.

Nevertheless, I am persuaded that a general ought not to be inattentive to the advice of even a subaltern officer, as it is the duty of a good citizen to forget himself when the welfare of his country is at stake, and not regard who furnishes the advice that may be productive of happy, wished-for consequences.

ARTICLE XXVI.

Of the Maneuvers of an Army

It will be seen by the maxims which I have laid down in this work, on what the theory turns of those evolutions which I have introduced amongst my troops. The object of these maneuvers is to gain time on every occasion, and decide an affair more quickly than has heretofore been the custom; and, in short, to overset the enemy by the furious shocks of our cavalry. By means of this impetuosity, the coward is hurried away, and obliged to do his duty as well as the bravest; no single trooper can be useless. The whole depends on the spirit of the attack.

I therefore flatter myself that every general, convinced of the necessity and advantage of discipline, will do every thing in his power to preserve and improve it, both in time of war and of peace.

The enthusiastic speech made by Vegece respecting the Romans, will never leave my memory: "And at length," says he, "the Roman discipline triumphed over the hordes of Germans, the force of the Gauls, the German cunning, the barbarian swarm, and subdued the whole universe." So much does the prosperity of a state depend on the discipline of its army.

ARTICLE XXVII.

Of Winter Quarters

When a campaign is ended, we think of winter quarters, which must be arranged according to the circumstances in which we find ourselves.

The first thing to be done is the forming the chain of troops who are to cover these quarters, which may be effected in three different ways, either behind a river, taking advantage of posts that are defended by mountains, or under the protection of some fortified towns.

In the year 1741-2, my troops who wintered in Bohemia, took up their position behind the Elbe. The chain which covered them began at Brandeis, and extending along by Nienbourg, Koelin, Pojebrod, and Pardubitz, ended at Konigingraetz.

I must add here, that rivers must not be too much confided in, as when frozen they can be crossed at any point. Care should be taken to post hussars in every part of the chain to watch the enemy's movements, for which purpose, they should patrol frequently in front to observe if all be quiet, or if the enemy be assembling troops.

Besides the chain of infantry, there should be placed also brigades of cavalry and infantry here and there, to be in readiness to lend assistance wherever it might be wanted.

In the winter of 1744-5, the chain of quarters was formed the whole length of those mountains which separate Silesia from Bohemia, and we guarded very particularly the frontiers of our quarters, that we might remain quiet.

Lieutenant-General de Trusches had to take charge of the front of Lusatia as far as the country of Glatz, the town of Sagan, and the posts from Schmiedberg to Friedland, which last place was fortified by redoubts. There were also some other small entrenched posts on the roads of Schatzlar, Liebau, and Silberberg. The general had likewise contrived a reserve to support that post which might be first insulted by the enemy. All these detachments were covered by abbatis made in the woods, and all the roads leading into Bohemia were rendered impassible. Every post was also supplied with hussars, for the purpose of reconnoitering.

General Lehwald covered the country of Glatz with a detachment of the same nature, and with the same prudent cautions. These two generals lent each other assistance in such a way, that if the Austrians had marched against General

Trusches, General Lehwald would have entered Bohemia to take the enemy in the rear, and Trusches would have returned the favor had Lehwald been attacked.

The towns of Tropau and Jagerndorf were our biggest points in Upper Silesia, and the communication was by way of Zeigenhals and Patchskau to Glatz, and by Neustadt to Neiss.

It must be observed here, that we are not to trust too much to the security of mountains, but remember the proverb, "that wherever a goat can pass a soldier can."

With regard to the chains of quarters that are supported by fortresses, I refer you to the winter quarters of Marshal Saxe. They are the best, but it is not in our power to choose, as the chain must be made according to the nature of the ground which we occupy.

I shall lay it down here as a maxim, that we are never to fancy ourselves perfectly secure from the enemy's annoyance in any one town or post, but that our attention must be constantly alive to the keeping of winter quarters quiet.

Another maxim to be observed in winter quarters is to distribute the regiments by brigades, that they may be always under the eyes of the generals.

Our service also requires, that the generals

should, if possible be with their own regiments: but there may be exceptions to this rule, of which the general commanding the army will be the best judge.

Here follow the rules that are to be observed respecting the maintenance of troops in winter quarters.

If circumstances absolutely require that we take up winter quarters in our own country, the captains and subaltern officers are to receive a gratuity proportionate to the common allowance which they receive in winter quarters. This is to be furnished with his bread and meat at free cost.

But if the winter quarters are in an enemy's country, the general-in-chief of the troops shall receive 15,000 florins, the generals of the cavalry and infantry 10,000 each, lieutenant-generals 7000, major-generals (camp marshals) 5000, captains of cavalry 2000, of infantry 1800, and the subaltern officers 1000 ducats or from 4 to 500 florins. The country is to supply the soldier with bread, flesh, and beer gratis, but he is to have no money, as that only tends to favor desertion.

The general-in-chief is to take care that this business be properly arranged, and that no pillaging be allowed, but he is not to be too strict with an officer who has it in his power to make any trifling, fair advantage.

If the army be quartered in an enemy's country, it is the duty of the general commanding to see that the necessary number of recruits be furnished (such distribution should obtain in the circles, that three regiments, for example, should be assigned to one, and four to the other). Each circle should also be subdivided into regiments, as is done in the enrolling cantonments.

If the recruits are furnished voluntarily by the states of the country, so much the better; if not, compulsory methods must be used. They ought to arrive very early, that the officer may have time to drill them and make them fit for duty the following spring. This, however, is not to prevent the captain from sending out recruiting parties.

As the general-in-chief ought to interest himself in the whole of this economy, he should be particularly careful that the artillery horses and the provisions, which are a tribute of the country, are furnished in kind or in hard cash.

All the baggage wagons, and in short, the whole apparatus of an army, is also to be repaired at the enemy's cost.

Minute attention must be paid by the general that the cavalry officers repair their saddles, bridles, stirrups, and boots, and that the officers of infantry provide their men with shoes, stockings, shirts, and gaitres for the ensuing campaign. The soldiers' blankets and tents should also be repaired, the cavalry swords filed, and the arms of the infantry put in good condition. The artillery, likewise, must prepare the necessary quantity of cartridges for the infantry.

It still remains to be seen by the general, that the troops which form the chain are well provided with powder and ball, and in short, that nothing be wanting in the whole army.

If time allows, the general would do well to visit some of his quarters, to examine into the state of the troops, and satisfy himself that the officers attend to the exercising of their men, as well as to every other part of their duty; for it is necessary that the old soldiers should be employed in this way as well as the recruits, in order to keep them in practice.

At the beginning of a campaign, we change the cantoning quarters, and distribute them according to the order of battle, viz. the cavalry on the wings, and the infantry in the center. These cantonments generally extend nine or ten leagues (from four to five miles) in front, to four (two) in depth, and when the time of encamping draws near, they are to be contracted a little.

I find it very convenient in cantonments to distribute the troops under the orders of the six eldest generals: one, for example, shall command all the cavalry of the right wing, and another that of the left, in the first line, whilst two others shall command that of the second. In this method, all orders will more quickly be executed, and the troops be more easily formed into columns to go to camp.

On the subject of winter quarters, I must again advise you to be very careful of not going into them before you are well convinced that the enemy's army is entirely separated. Keep always in your recollection the misfortune which befel the Elector Frederick William, when he was surprised by the Marshal de Turenne in his quarters at Alsace.

ARTICLE XXVIII.

Of Winter Campaigns in Particular

Winter campaigns ruin the troops, both on account of the diseases which they occasion, and by obliging them to be constantly in motion, which prevents their being well clothed or recruited. The same inconvenience attends the carriage of ammunition and provisions. It is certain that the best army in the world cannot long support campaigns of this kind, for which reason they ought ever to be avoided, as being, of all expeditions, the most to be condemned. Accidents, however, may occur, which will oblige a general to undertake them.

I believe that I have made more winter campaigns than any general of this age, and that I shall do right to explain the motives which induced me to such undertakings.

At the death of the Emperor Charles VI in the year 1740, there were but two Austrian regiments in all Silesia. Having determined to make good the claims of my house on that duchy, I was obliged to make war in winter, that I might profit by every favorable circumstance, and carry the theater of war to the Neiss.

If I had delayed my project till the spring, the war would have been established between Crossen and Glogau, and it would have required three or four hard campaigns to effect that which we accomplished by one simple march. This reason appeared to me sufficiently cogent.

If I did not succeed in the winter campaign which I made in the year 1742 to relieve the country from the Elector of Bavaria, it was because the French behaved like fools, and the Saxons like traitors.

My third winter campaign in the year 1741-2 was forced upon me, as I was obliged to drive the Austrians from Silesia, which they had invaded.

From the beginning of the winter 1745-6, the Austrians and Saxons wished to introduce themselves into my hereditary dominions, that they might put every thing to fire and sword.I acted according to my usual principle, and got the start of them by making war in the middle of winter in the very heart of their own country.

Should similar circumstances occur, I should not hesitate to pursue the same plan, and shall applaud the conduct of my generals who shall follow my example. But I must ever blame those who, without the concurrence of such reasons, shall undertake a war at that season of the year.

In regard to the detail of winter campaign, the troops are always to be as close to each other as possible in their cantonments, and two or three regiments of cavalry, mixed with infantry, should be lodged in one village, if it be large enough to hold them. Sometimes all the infantry are quartered in one town, as the Prince of Anhalt did at Torgau, Eilenbourg, Meissen, and two or three other small towns (whose names I forget) in Saxony, after which he encamped himself.

When we come near the enemy, a rendezvous is to be appointed to the troops, who are to continue marching as before in several columns; and when about to make any decisive movement, such as, storming the enemy's quarters, or marching against him to engage, we arrange ourselves in order of battle, remaining under the canopy of heaven, each company kindling a large fire, by which to pass away the night. But as such fatigues are too distressing to be long endured, all possible dispatch should be employed in enterprises of this nature. We must not stand contemplating our danger or hesitating about it, but form our resolution with spirit and execute it with firmness.

Be careful of undertaking a winter campaign in a country which is crowded with fortified places, for the season will prevent your setting down seriously before a place which you cannot carry by surprise. We may be assured beforehand that such project will miscarry, as it is morally impossible it should be otherwise.

If it be left to our choice, the troops should have as much rest during the winter as possible, and the time should be employed to the best advantage in recovering the army, that at the opening of the campaign they may get the start of their adversaries.

These are nearly the principal rules of the grand maneuvers of war, the particulars of which have been explained as much as was in my power. I have taken particular care that what I have said should be clear and intelligible, but if any parts should, in your idea, still remain obscure, I shall be favored by your communicating them, that I may either explain myself more fully, or subscribe to your opinion, if it prove better than mine own.

The small experience of war which has fallen to my share, convinces me that it is an art never to be exhausted, but that something new will ever reward his labor who studies it with serious application.

I shall not think my moments misemployed, if what I have said should stimulate my officers to the study of that science, which will afford them the most certain opportunity of acquiring glory, rescuing their names from the rust of oblivion, and securing by their brilliant actions a glorious and immortal fame.